It Is Finished

An examination of Roman Catholicism in light of
scripture and the facts of History

By Joe Loeschnig

To Vickie...

My beautiful wife of 38 years,

...and the children,

Joseph
Ciara
Jochanan
Cerrissa
Joe
Diane
Sue

Table of Contents

Introduction

"All men are like grass,

And all their glory is like the flowers of the field;

The grass withers and the flowers fall,

But the Word of the Lord stands forever."

I Peter 1:24

It has been well over thirty years since a merciful and compassionate God opened my eyes and set me free from the labyrinth of the gospel of sacramental grace and the convoluted theology of Roman Catholicism.

It is never a good idea to deride anyone whom God refers to as "his people" (Rev. 18:4). On the other hand, I would be remiss if I did not wholeheartedly encourage my brothers and sisters in Christ to make a swift departure from any church where truth is nowhere to be found.

Our creator has blessed us with a free will, we can use it to reside in any neighborhood we choose, if we are unaware the neighborhood we choose is located in a major flood zone and a former resident feels compelled to warn us of the impending danger, we can choose to listen and investigate the truth of what he has to say, or we can tell him to get lost, it's none of his business where we choose to reside.

Preface

All the religions of the world ignore man's inherent inability to establish his righteousness before a Holy God apart from the cross, but there is only one world religion that has, for centuries, embellished and usurped God's finished work for the salvation of mankind.

Catholicism is not built on the rock, which is Christ, but on the false foundation that an elite and self-anointed group of sinful men have been given God's authority to administer His grace to a lost and dying world.

In recent years the Church of Rome has been plagued with accusations that some members of her royal priesthood have been sexually molesting the children of her faithful, her pundits are quick to point out the reasons for the abuse; left-wingers have planted pedophiles in the priestly ranks to undermine Christianity, there are too many gay priests, her bishops are to blame. Her real problem is not the left wingers, gay priests, or her bishops. It is the same problem we must all face sooner or later. It is a sin problem—a problem that she has no power to fix.

The only remedy for our sin problem is faith in Jesus Christ and His all-sufficient sacrifice of the cross.

1

Roman Catholicism: A Metamorphisis

"My kingdom is not of this world."

John 18:36

"They are not of the world anymore than I am of the world."

John 17:14

The Church Triumphant (AD 311)

"After hacking his rivals to pieces, Constantine decided to make the God of the Christians his God and the God of his empire. Instead of placing Miltiades in chains, Constantine embraced him and draped the purple robe of a high priest around the old bishops shoulders. Miltiades was befuddled.

"What was transpiring before him was too bizarre to be true! Two worlds had collided. The world of Caesar with its riches and power, its pomp and splendor, was a world to be shunned. The world of Christ was a world of poverty and service, of persecution and self denial.

"The dumbstruck Miltiades merely nodded as the emperor

rambled about the great sign in the sky that was now engraved on the shields of his soldiers. The old man refused to utter a word, even though the emperor appeared to confuse Jesus Christ, the suffering servant of the scriptures with Sol, the Roman god of the sun." [1]

Perhaps tens of millions might have been spared hundreds of years of religious tyranny and persecution had Miltiades simply responded: "O great Emperor, your kingdom is of this world, the Kingdom of Christ is not of this world."

The stage was set, and the door was now wide open. The gospel the apostle Paul preached, the gospel of God's grace through faith in Jesus and His finished work of the cross would now become the Gospel of Rome.

Her faithful subjects would now be required to submit to the law of the New Testament, and they would be bound by the Gospel of sacramental grace. A new king would arise: 'Pontifex Maximus,' 'The most holy father,' 'Vicar of Christ,' 'The Pope."

"Go into all the world and preach the gospel to all creation."
Mark 16:15

Since Christianity was now the official state religion and the days of persecution and suffering for Christ and His Gospel were over, why preach the good news to all creation when you now had the power and authority to force the gospel of sacramental grace down the throats of all mankind.

Holy Father, protect them by the power of your name,: -- when I was with them, I protected them and kept them safe by that name you gave me... They are not of the world any more than I am of the world.
John 17:11,14

Her New Protector

"The emperor's duty was to act as a protector of the Roman Church"—John VIII (882Ad) advanced the cause of papal supremacy by successfully asserting the right of the popes not only to crown but also to choose the emperor." [2]

"What fellowship can light have with darkness?"
II Corinthians 6:14

"As Christianity flourished under his protection (Constantine) simple spacious buildings were no longer sufficient. Millions of pagans suddenly entered the church, and some of their customs inevitably crept into the liturgy"

"The use of the kiss as a sign of reverence for holy objects. 'The use of candles', 'devotion to relics,' 'incense,' 'facing the east when praying,' 'The practice of genuflection.'" [3]

"Adoration of the Eucharist, whether in the tabernacle or exposed on the altar is to be venerated by genuflecting on one knee." [4]

"You say, 'I am rich; I have acquired wealth and do not need a thing, but you do not realize that you are wretched, pitiful, poor and naked."

Revelation 3:17

"Rome enjoyed certain attributes that raised it above all the other churches and destined it for a unique roll as a center of church unity—it became a very wealthy church." [5]

"Before the peace of Constantine (AD 313) the church's properties were very limited, but after his reign, by his gifts and those of newly converted nobles, the church found herself possessing large estates. About AD 600 the pope might have been called the largest land proprietor in the world." [6]

I promised you to one husband, to Christ, so that I might present you as a pure virgin to Him. But I am afraid that just as Eve was deceived by the serpent's cunning, your minds may somehow be led astray from your pure devotion to Christ.

II Corinthians 11:2,3

Now that the Church of Rome had consummated her spiritual fornication with the kings of the earth, she would make the world an offer it could not refuse.

"Do not repay evil with evil or insult with insult, but with blessing, because to this you were called so that you may inherit a blessing."

I Peter 3:9 (The first Pope!)

"By 1808, when the Inquisition was abolished, its victims numbered, according to the historian named before, 31,912 persons burned alive, and 291,450 imprisoned in its dungeons. [7]

"In addition to eight crusades, the popes also played a leading part in the Italian wars of the 16th century." [8]

The most 'Holy Fathers' of the church triumphant continually offered spiritual blessings to anyone who took up arms to butcher the enemies of the Church of Rome. Holy wars were not exactly what Christ had in mind when he taught his disciples, "Blessed are the peacemakers," "Love your enemies and pray for those who persecute you."

"The church would never be the same again after the Emperor converted it became fashionable to be Christian, in fact, the opposite form of persecution took place against the pagans." [9]

2

Her 'Most Holy Fathers'

Rome would like everyone to believe that with the exception of a few bad popes, that she calls 'scoundrels,' her 'Holy Fathers' were humble peace loving men who desired nothing more than to share the gospel of Christ with a lost and dying world. Never mind the fact the doctrines of her 'scoundrel' popes are just as infallible and binding on her faithful today as they were during the reigns of the Borgia and Medici families.

Rome's insistence that her faithful are bound by the doctrine and teaching of men who possessed the moral integrity of 'Jack the Ripper' is based on the myth that every pope is Peter's successor, and Christ appointed Peter the first pope and handed him the keys to heaven.

If we can learn anything from Peter's successors it is this: Too much power concentrated in the hands of one man inevitably leads to corruption. When sinful men elevate sinful men to god-like status, the inevitable result is ruthless tyranny and unrestrained corruption.

Who is the greatest in the kingdom of heaven?" "I tell you the truth, unless you change and become like little children, you will never enter the kingdom of heaven."

Matthew 18: 1,3,4

Are we to actually believe that the Jesus of the Bible is ecstatic knowing the successors of Peter are now referred to as "Pontifex Maximus", "Supreme Pontiff," "Most Holy Fathers"?

Is it possible that Peter, Rome's first pope, can be looking down from heaven, observing his successors while they sit on their earthly thrones, ruling over their earthly kingdoms, adorned in flowing robes of scarlet and purple, and thinking: "Wow!" I got it wrong when I wrote to the church!"

"All men are like grass, and all their glory like the flowers of the field; the grass withers and the flowers fall, but the word of the Lord stands forever."

I Peter 1:24, 25

"God opposes the proud but gives grace to the humble, humble yourselves, therefore, under God's mighty hand, that He may lift you up in due time."

I Peter 5:5,6

Paul, writing to the church circa 60 A.D.:

"Do not think of yourself more highly than you ought."

Romans 12:3

"If anyone thinks he is something when he is nothing, he deceives himself."

Galatians 6:3

Peter, the First Pope

"Apart from me you can do nothing."

John 15:5

Only Jesus knows how vulnerable our flesh can be to the powers of darkness, When He tried to explain to Peter and the other disciples that He must go to Jerusalem and suffer many things at the hands of elders, chief priests, and teachers of the law, and that he must be killed and on the third day be raised to life, Peter had a 'knee-jerk' reaction. "Never Lord," he said, "This shall never happen to you." Jesus turned and said to Peter:

Get behind me Satan, you are a stumbling block to me; you do not have in mind the things of God, but the things of men.

Matthew 16:22,23

This was no classic case of demon possession, this was an example of how vulnerable we become when we take our eyes off of Jesus and the power of His cross to focus on self and the power of our flesh.

Peter, Bishop of Rome
The Distortion of the Historical Facts

Sacred Apostolic Tradition or Roman Catholic Invention?

"That Peter founded the church in Rome is extremely doubtful and that he served as its first bishop (as we understand the term today) for even one year, much less the twenty-five year period that is claimed for him, is an unfounded tradition that can be traced back to a point no earlier than the third century. The liturgical celebrations which relate to the ascent of Peter to the Roman episcopy do not begin to make their appearance until the fourth century at the earliest. Furthermore, there is no mention of the Roman Episcopy of Peter in the New Testament, I Clement, or the epistles of Ignatius. The tradition is only dimly discerned in Hegesippus and may be implied in the suspect letter of Dionysius of Corinth to the Romans (C170). By the third century, however, the early assumptions based upon invention or vague unfounded tradition have been transformed into facts of history." [10]

"There is no unequivocal evidence about the status of the pope in the earliest days of the church—non-Catholic historians in general contend that the bishop of Rome was accorded honor over the other bishops, not authority." [11]

"It may be true, as some historians say, that the council of Nicea (325) knew nothing of the doctrine of papal supremacy." [12]

Popes will be Popes

"If you love me, keep my commandments."(New King James Version)

John 14:15

In defense of her "scoundrel" popes and their "sound doctrine," Catholic theologians, Rev. Trigilio, Jr. and Rev Kenneth Brighenti, offer the following to the "faithful":

"As bad and as evil as some of the scoundrels were (members of the Borgia and Medici families for example) committing sins of fornication, adultery, murder, theft, greed and violence, not one of them ever tried to eliminate one of the commandments, nor did any of them attempt to convince the faithful that their personal sinfulness was something to imitate." Or to put it another way, "God may have anointed our 'Holy Fathers' with supreme moral teaching authority over the whole world, but you better not imitate their behavior."

It's All a Mystery

"All the faithful must believe that the Apostolic See and the Roman pontiff hold primacy over the whole world."

"By virtue of his office, the Roman pontiff possesses infallibility in teaching when as the supreme pastor and teacher of all Christian faithful he proclaims by definitive act that a doctrine of faith or morals is to be held."

"There have been several bad Popes in history, yet their immoral behavior was never promoted or deemed acceptable by the church." [13]

When the Catholic Church declares that the immoral behavior of her evil popes was never acceptable but their teaching and doctrine on morality can be infallible, there can be only one logical explanation; "It's all a mystery!"

What Jesus said is not exactly what he meant.

According to Catholic theologians Brighenti and Trigilio, Jesus' command in Matthew 23:9 not to call anyone on earth 'Father' only applied to the Rabbinical teachers of Jesus day, their reasoning, "They often fought with each other, furthermore they did not act like spiritual fathers who loved and cared for their spiritual children." [14]

<u>Schism of the West:</u> "The church was torn apart from top to bottom by the schism, it was impossible to know to whom allegiance was due" –(the schism) which lasted with its two lines of popes (and sometimes three)" [15]

<u>Schism of the East:</u> "The origins, causes and developments of the schism are matters of much complication, still not fully unraveled." [16]

<u>Meletian Schism:</u> "A schism against St. Peter, Archbishop of Alexandria by Meletius, Bishop of Lycopolis." [17]

It would be an understatement to say the (not so) Holy Fathers of Rome often fought with each other! Caring for and loving their spiritual children was not exactly the fruit for which they were known!

"By their fruit you will recognize them."

Matthew 7:20

"The plots, counterplots, bribes, threats, choreographed violence, and shifting alliances that centered on the prize of the papacy in Rome and central Italy during this period almost defy description." [18]

"In the past centuries when the popes were head of papal states, electoral politics involved bribes, threats, poisons and even fist fights in the conclave." [19]

"Everyone was conscious of the evil state of affairs caused by the great schism (evil popes, evil clergy, and evil Roman Curia) degradation of the papacy, exorbitant demands of the rival papal tax collectors, breakdown of church courts, ignorance, immorality of the clergy, simony everywhere, most blatantly in the Roman Curia, whose excessive dispensations and indulgences were the scandal of Europe." [20]

Simony (Spiritual Prostitution)

The popes had gained control of a large number of ecclesiastical appointments, and the sale was a lucrative and even necessary source of papal income.

"By the time of Leo X (1521) it is estimated that there were some two thousand marketable church jobs, which were literally sold over the counter at the Vatican; even a cardinal's hat might go to the highest bidder." [21]

"The papacy wallowed in corruption unparalleled since the tenth century." [22]

"Under Constantine the church was firmly set on the road to union with the state—This alliance with the state profoundly influenced every aspect of the church's thought and life." [23]

The Council at Jerusalem A.D. 51

In attendance and presiding at the first church council (ironically called to refute those who were trying to add law to the gospel of grace(Paul, Barnabas, Peter, James, the apostles and elders, not presiding and noticeably absent, Caesar!

The God Fathers of Rome
Sylvester I (The Absentee Pope)

"During his lifetime Constantine dominated the church to such a extent that little is known of Sylvester beyond the name of his father—the date of his election (January 314), and the date of his death."

"A council was called at Aries in 314, just ten months after the gathering in Rome. Though Sylvester did not travel to Aries—the meeting was important.

"Anxious as always about the unity of his empire, Constantine summoned a great council to meet at Nicea in 325. There were some 250 bishops present at Nicea, there were a handful from the west including Hosius, bishop of Cordova, who acted as the emperor's personal representative, two priests attended in place of pope Sylvester.

"Proceedings were conducted like the Roman Senate"—"the emperor sometimes presided." [24]

Damasus I 366-384

Not exactly a 'Holy Father' who turned the other cheek. Damasus would have nothing to do with relinquishing his crown to arch rival and anti-pope, Ursinus. He acted more like Genghis Khan than the Vicar of Christ, he put his savior's commands on the back burner while he systematically destroyed his enemies with the ruthlessness of Attila the Hun.

"Battles broke out between supporters of the rival popes—the seven priests remained and set up a separate church, much to Damasus' irritation."—"Damasus hired gangs of thugs to drive them out. There was a great battle around the basilica in October, 366 which left 150 people dead."—"So Damasus destroyed his enemies by using violence in the age of violence."—"Penitent Arians were being received back into the church—they even had their own bishop, and their own very popular holy man called Macarius—they were a threat to Damasus, he appealed to the imperial authorities for help as well as using his own gang of thugs, in the ensuing brawl Macarius was so badly beaten that he died of his wounds." [25]

"Damasus earned criticism for his lavish lifestyle and for currying favor with the old Roman Aristocrats, especially the woman, many of whom were still pagans. At one point he had to defend himself against charges of adultery." [26]

For no one can lay any foundation other than the one already laid, which is Jesus Christ. If anyone builds on this foundation using gold, silver, costly stones, wood, hay or straw, his work will be shown for what it is, because the day will bring it to light, it will be revealed with fire and the fire will test the quality of each man's work."

I Corinthians 3:11-13

Sixtus III 432-440

"His particular glory was to preside over the restoration of the city of Rome to something like the splendor it had enjoyed before the pillaging by Alaric's warriors. His greatest moment can still be seen today: It is the magnificent Basilica of Santa Maria Maggiore—now that the pope had replaced the emperor as Rome's leading personage, that point was to be driven home by the construction of Christian Churches." [27]

My kingdom is not of this world."

John 18:36

Set your hearts on things above where Christ is seated at the right hand of God. Set your minds on things above, not on earthly things."

Colossians 3:1,2

By the same word the present heavens and earth are reserved for fire—but in keeping with his promise we are looking forward to a new heaven and a new earth, the home of righteousness.

II Peter 3:7,13

Leo I 440-461

"Leo appropriated the once pagan title. 'Pontifex Maximus,' still used by the popes today and born, until the end of the fourth century, by Roman emperors to indicate that as civil rulers they had a right to intervene in religious affairs—with Leo, however, the position was reversed. He was a religious leader who intervened in civil affairs. Leo voiced a new view of the role of the city of Rome. As Romulus and Remus had founded the city—so Peter and Paul had re-founded it—by the end of Leo's episcopate or pontificate, as it was now called since he had adopted the title 'Pontifex Maximus,' the pope had replaced the emperor as the most important figure in the city of Rome." [28]

"Leo continued Sixtus' policy of building, renovating and ornamenting the Basilicas and churches of the city, and he seems to have paid special attention to those in some way linked with the name of the Emperor Constantine." [32]

"Far from decrying Rome as the unspeakably corrupt 'Babylon' which Peter loathed, Leo apostrophized the city. 'Rome! You holy family! You chosen people! You priestly and royal city! You have become the capital of the world by being Peters see…you have extended your rule far and wide over land and sea…your empire of peace is greater than the old Roman military empire." [33]

John II 530-532 (Pope Mercury)

"His given name was 'Mercury' from a pagan Roman god, upon becoming pope he took the name 'John' rather than Pope Mercury." [34]

According to Catholic theologians, "Relics of the saints have nothing to do with Vincent Price, Halloween or the Macabre." [29]

Boniface IV 608-615

"When Pope Boniface IV consecrated the old Roman Pantheon as Santa Maria Rotondo in 610, he had thirty-two wagon loads of martyrs' bones brought from the catacombs and placed in the various shrines within the newly consecrated church—the physical relics of their dead holy people became important to Christians— that they were essentially all phony is not the issue, the point is that people believed in them." [30]

Lifting up Charlemagne to a Lost and Dying World
Stephen IV 816-817

"A Roman Aristocrat [he] was firmly devoted to the house of

Charlemagne, almost immediately after his election he made the people of Rome swear allegiance to Louis, the pious Charlemagne's son." [31]

Stephen VI 885-891 (Pope Psycho)

"After his death in 896, Formosus' decaying corpse was dug up, dressed in pontifical robes, and put on trial by his successor, Stephen VI"—"His body was tossed in the Tiber, minus the three fingers of his right hand that he used to bless the crowds and sign documents." [35]

Sergius III 904-911 (The Assassin)

"Cardinal Sergius, who assassinated both Leo and Christopher in prison, together with all the other cardinals who opposed him, had his enemies at the papal court strangled and himself declared Pope Sergius III. In 906, when Sergius had been pope for two years, Marozia, aged fifteen, became his mistress, they had only one child, John (subsequently Pope John XI)" [36]

John XI 931-936

"The family had little trouble manipulating the papacy for decades. John XI for example, was reputed to be the son of Pope Sergius III and Theophylacts 13 year old daughter." [37]

John XII 955-964 (Pope Playboy)

"Scandalized even the Roman society of his day with his addiction to pleasure and debauchery—looked on the papacy as a means of enjoying life to the full—chief pleasures were women and hunting—his ignorance was startling—deposed for his immorality." [38]

"Surrounded by boys and girls his own age and rank, he spent his days and nights eating sumptuously, playing at the tables, hunting, and in love affairs. The Pope's palace was frequented by courtesans and prostitutes." [39]

Understandably 'Holy Father' John reminded the Roman elite too much of themselves; "In 963 the Romans took an oath not to elect another pope without imperial consent." [40]

Although deposed, John was not to be easily denied. Leo VIII was chosen by the Emperor to replace John, but as soon as Otto, the King of the Saxons had left Rome, John came back. He wreaked terrible vengeance on his adversaries. Pope Leo took refuge with the Emperor. In the meantime, the Romans elected Benedict V, the Emperor hurried back to Rome, deposed Benedict and reinstated Leo. But alas, 'Holy Father' John, on his way to visit his mistress had been murdered." [41]

"The papacy reached a high point of corruption in the 10th century, when the Holy See was cynically bought and sold." [42]

It always helps to have relatives in high places.

John XIX 1024-1033

"When Benedict died in 1024, his family convinced and bribed electors to get his younger brother, John XIX, elected, who in a single day was elevated from layman to Pope of Rome." [43]

Gregory VI 1045-1046

"As the toy of the Roman nobility, the papacy once more went into decline after his death (Pope Sylvester), it reached such an appalling state that one Roman priest seems to have bought the office from Benedict IX."—"But this pope, Gregory VI, though a great improvement on those who had gone before, could not free himself from the taint of Simony." [44]

Benedict IX 1047-1048

(The Boy Pope)

"When John XIX died under suspicious circumstances in 1033, a relative of John's took his own twelve year old son, also called Theophylact, had papal clothes made to fit him, lifted him bodily onto the papal throne, and had him consecrated Pope as Benedict IX. The spectacle of this twelve year old issuing excommunications, giving his papal blessing, formulating decrees, consecrating bishops, deciding theological matters, was ludicrous enough, but it took more than that to shake the impassive Greeks." [45]

Leo IX 1049-1054 (Pope Rambo)

After deposing Gregory VI, Henry III of Germany appointed his relative, Bruno to the papacy, he became Pope Leo IX.

"When his attempts to reconcile the warring factions among the Roman nobility failed, he resorted to brutal force. The lands of the Crescentii and Theophylacts were laid waste, their towns destroyed and their vines uprooted."—"He was equally ruthless with church men." [46]

Honorius II 1124-1130 (King of the Cage)

"Theobaldo was unanimously elected pope in 1124. While the installation was in progress, the Frangipani family broke into the assembly and at sword-point had cardinal Lamberto of Ostia acclaimed pope."—"There was a violent struggle in which Theobaldo suffered blows and severe wounds, but the outcome was that he was either forced or persuaded to resign while Lamberto was elected and installed as Honorius II." [47]

Innocent III 1198-1216 (Maybe not so Innocent!)

"First pope to apply force on a considerable scale to suppress religious opinions." [48]

Gregory IX 1227-1241 (The Inquisitor General)

"The pontifical inquisition was a church (ecclesiastical) court that was established by Pope Gregory IX in 1230 to root out heresy."—"Hersey is false teaching which can threaten the very foundation of the church."—"The accused were generally given a month to recant. If they did not, then a public trial was held, and if they were found guilty and still did not renounce their false teachings, they would be handed over to civil authority, which usually meant death. Most people conjure thoughts about the inquisition as agents of torture, and unfortunately, this is not far from the truth." (Catholic Theologians) [49]

Innocent IV 1243-1254
(Torture permitted, but only as a last resort)

"Pope Innocent IV in a papal bull permitted torture as a last resort in extreme cases in order to smash the stubbornness of the heretic and force them to admit guilt. The painful extraction of confessions only occurred after a church tribunal had enough proof and evidence that the accused were in fact guilty." (Catholic Theologians) [50]

Boniface VIII 1294-1303
(He will make the world an offer it can't refuse)

"We declare, say, define and pronounce that it is absolutely necessary for the salvation of every human creature to be subject to the Roman Pontiff." (Papal bull, "Unum Sanctum") (Emphasis added)

"Apart from individual killings and torturings, he will wipe out one whole town. In October 1298, he will have every man, woman, child and animal killed in the town of Palestrina—Boniface will shower the world with excommunications and anathemas and interdicts, will torture and massacre, will breed hate and jealousy. He will glory in his honors, be unsparing in his ferocity, and immovable in his sense of dignity." [51]

Clement V 1305-1314 (A Blind Guide)

"You have neglected," Dante wrote in a letter to Clement V, "to guide the chariot of the bride of the crucified along the path so clearly marked for her."—"Clement's city and court of Avignon was home to wine, women, song, and priests who cavorted, Petrarch said, 'As if all their glory consisted not in Christ but in feasting and unchastity.' 'Wolves' screamed poet Alvaro Pelago, 'have become the masters of the church.' St. Cathrine of Sienna stated: 'At the papal court which ought to have been a paradise of virtue, my nostrils were assailed by the odor of hell.'" [52]

Finally, all of you, live in harmony with one another, be sympa-
thetic, love as brothers, be compassionate and humble. Do not
repay evil for evil or insult with insult.

I Peter 3:8,9

John XXII 1316-1334

"Glutted his hatred of Hughes Gerold, Bishop of Cahors, on a charge of conspiring against the life of the pope, he was delivered to the secular arm, and in July of the same year he was partially flayed alive and then dragged to the stake and burned." [53]

Urban VI 1378-1389

"Obstinate, obsessive, paranoid, and prone to violent outburst of temper, his behavior became so eccentric that some wondered if they had elected a deranged man. He had cardinals whom he accused of plotting against him tortured and put to death." [54]

"Urban turned more violent and savage suspecting his own cardinals of plotting against him, he put them to torture, and five of them died shortly afterward, probably thrown overboard from the pope's warship." [55]

"When he died in St Peter's, he will be described as 'the worst of men, cruel, most scandalous.'" [56]

Boniface IX 1389-1404
(For the right price, everyone can get the "Jubilee Indulgence")

"He conceived of another step in the indulgence procedure. Every so often the popes declare what is called a jubilee year. In that year, if the faithful visit Rome, say a certain amount of prayers, make a pilgrimage on foot to certain churches, they are believed to obtain an indulgence and remission of guilt. Boniface IX made one small adjustment: you needn't come to Rome—the majority of Catholics couldn't anyway—to get the plenary indulgence, stay at home, say certain prayers, visit certain designated churches in your area, pay a fixed sum, and you receive the jubilee indulgence.

"The sale of offices, which had always existed, took on a grand scale with Pope Benedict IX. Every job of scribe and minor clerk had a price. Higher positions, including that of cardinal, were priced and sold." [57]

"When Boniface died in 1404, his last words: 'If I had money, I would be alright.'" [58]

Catholic theologians Brighenti and Trigilio:

"All the faithful of Christ must believe that the apostolic see and the Roman pontiff hold primacy over the whole world, and the pontiff of Rome himself is the successor of blessed Peter, the chief of the apostles, and is the true vicar of Christ and head of the whole church and faith, and teacher of all Christians." [59]

Gregory XII 1406-1415

"He spent half his day eating and drinking, the other half making money or spending it. He pawned the Papal Tiara for 6000 florins to pay his debts from war and gambling. He sold books from the Vatican library. He sold Rome and the Roman estates of the church to King Ladislas of Naples." [60]

Brighenti and Trigilio: "By virtue of his office, the Roman pontiff possesses infallibility in teaching when as the supreme pastor and teacher of all the Christian faithful, who strengthens his brothers and sisters in the faith, he proclaims by definitive act that a doctrine of faith or morals is to be held." [61]

Martin V 1417-1431

"In the 15th century and the first half of the 16th [his successors] were chiefly interested in increasing the temporal power of the papacy—raising the fortunes of themselves and their relatives." [62]

Brighenti and Trigilio: "They may have had few or no scruples, yet they never taught as official doctrine a repeal of any of the moral laws of God. None ever taught that what they did was okay." [63]

Sylvester IV 1471-1484

"The new pope soon displayed a worldliness and ruthlessness that shocked even jaded contemporaries. At the request of Ferdinand of Aragon and Isabell of Castile, he established the Spanish Inquisition and put its operation into their hands." [64]

Innocent VIII 1484-1492

"Under him the moral caliber of the papal courts sank even lower." [65]

Alexander VI 1492-1503

"Almost a synonym for a degenerate pope, he fathered nine children by different women and most scandalous, two while he was pope." [66]

"When Pope Alexander VI, the father of Lucrezia Borgia, marked the final victory of Catholic Spain over the Moors, he did so not with a mass at St. Peter's but with a party in the Piazza in front of the church. Flagons of wine flowed among the honored guests, women from Rome's most elegant brothels offered their services, and children were passed freely among bishops and priests celebrating Catholicism's latest triumph with a sexual bacchanalia." [67]

Leo X 1513-1521

"While pope, he employed 683 servants, including a keeper of the papal elephant." [68]

"[He] was preoccupied with Italian affairs and had no interest in theology anyway, turned a deaf ear to Luther's humble appeal of May 30, 1518, summoned Luther to appear in Rome within 60 days to answer the charge of heresy—the official documents accompanying the summons contained not even the barest recognition of the undeniable abuses connected with the indulgence system but instead an incredible tirade: 'Luther was a leper, a dog and the son of a bitch.'" [69]

"Even before his election as pope he lost 8,000 ducats a month at cards and another 8,000 on a popular lottery game called 'Primiera'"—"As pope, he is the same, only more so."—'We begin gloriously, we live gloriously, we die gloriously,' –a favorite phrase of Leo's." [70]

Clement VII 1523-1534

"The terrible cold-blooded massacre of Cesena was his most conspicuous exploit, but equally characteristic of the man was his threat to the citizens of Bologna that he would wash his hands and feet in their blood." [71]

Paul III 1534-1549

"In his younger days as a cardinal, he had behaved like many of his peers and begot three sons and a daughter. But in 1513 he broke with his mistress. He tipped his hand almost immediately after his election when he nominated two of his teenage grandchildren as cardinals. In 1542 Paul moved decisively to stop the spread of Lutheranism in Italy when he established the Roman Inquisition." [72]

Julius III 1550-1555

"Emotionally detached from the great moral and religious issues of the day"—"As his pontificate wound down he spent more and more time hunting, banqueting, attending the theater or simply passing his days in quiet luxury in the residence he had built for himself. His insistence on raising to the cardinate a shifty street urchin, age fifteen, was the great scandal of his pontificate. After Julius' death, that cardinal's crimes caught up with him, and he ended his days in prison." [73]

Paul IV 1555-1559

"He infused the Roman Inquisition with a new zealotry—he published the first papal 'Index of Forbidden Books,' so extreme and categorical in its strictures that Saint Peter Canisius, a contemporary who was certainly not soft on heresy, called it intolerable and a scandal. Seeing the Jews as a source of disbelief, he erected for the first time in Rome a ghetto and had them herded into it." [74]

Sixtus V 1585-1590

"A man of big ideas, though some of them—like his plans to conquer Egypt—were too ambitious to carry out. He showed the sternness of his nature by the ruthless measures he took against the bandits who infested the papal states. A report from Rome stated that there were more bandits heads exposed on the bridge of St. Angelo than melons sold in the markets, on the other hand, he was less severe in his treatment of crimes against the faith. Only five persons were executed for this reason—three of them priests who were burned at the stake." [75]

The Renaissance Papacy

The holy fathers of the renaissance papacy ruled over the church with the same diligence and ruthlessness of their Roman masters. It was, "A time when the pope's were more concerned with Italian politics than the interest of the universal church. It was a time of papal grandeur as the popes made Rome a foremost center of the renaissance and inspired imperishable works of art that to this day adorn the Vatican. Morally and spiritually it was a time of terrible decline. In fact under such popes as Sixtus IV, Innocent VIII, and Alexander VI, the papacy wallowed in corruption unparalleled since the tenth century. These men virtually bought the Tiara and used it mainly for the furtherance of personal and dynastic interests—filling the College of Cardinals with relatives and unworthy candidates." [76]

"The moral tone of the papal court was a scandal to Christendom."—"The papacy of Sixtus IV, Innocent VIII, Alexander VI, Julius II, Leo X, Clement VII and Paul III was one of sensuous splendor." [77]

Pius IX 1846-1878 Tradition, I am Tradition
The Birth of Infallibility

"This is truly a difficult situation for the church," wrote Fr. Henri Icard, a sculpician priest from Paris, in his journal, "The most absolute power in the hands of a man who will only listen to the people who think—or rather, speak—the way he does."—"The pope deeply injured the bishops with his biting remarks more clearly than any words. However, Pius IX's outbursts of rage revealed just how ungovernably passionate his temperament was. His anger had been feared even back in Spoleto and Imola. As pope he did not improve in this area. Anyone who dared oppose this pet idea of his (infallibility) was made to feel his wrath."—"When Pius IX presided over the Vatican Council, he was already seventy eight years old. The pope's intellectual capacities were deteriorating—'He no longer has any memory from one day to the next,' remarked Bishop William Clifford. "Pius IX could no longer concentrate on a subject for any length of time and seemed to jump from one thing to the next."—"there are instances of near megalomania which are still hard to evaluate. In 1866, some years before the beginning of the council, Pius IX applied Christ's saying, 'I am the way, the truth and the life,' to himself. On February 8, 1871, count Harry Von Arnim-Suckow reported to the imperial chancellor, Prince Otto Von Bismarck of Pius IX's attempt to work a miracle, "The pope bade a cripple who was lying out in front, 'Rise up and walk!' but the experiment failed."—"The Catholic historian Franz Xavier Kraus noted in his diary: 'Apropos of PiusIX, Du Camp agrees with my view that ever since 1848 the pope has been both mentally ill and malicious." [78]

"In 1858 he kidnapped a six-year old Jewish boy in Bologna, took him to Rome and kept him there."—"How did a pope in the 19th century get into the kidnapping business? It happened because a young Christian woman in the papal state of Bologna told friends that she had secretly baptized a sick child, Edgardo Mortara, in the Jewish home where she was a servant. The child was only a year old at the time. The Inquisition in Bologna investigated the matter— very possibly at the instigation of Pius IX himself, according to the definitive three volume biography of Pius by Giacomo Martina S.J. when it was decided to believe the woman, despite problems with her story, the police were sent to take the boy (now six) away from his mother and father." [79]

Pius XI 1922-1939

"Helped to smooth Mussolini's way to power."—"The pope reaped his rewards when Mussolini signed the Lateran Concordat and treaty with the Vatican in 1929, the treaty granted the pope a magnificent sum of money. Pius tenure coincided with the rise of dictators to power in many other European states and as with Mussolini he did not hesitate to come to terms with them, even when it meant sacrificing Catholic political parties." [80]

"The Catholic center party decided it could not be rejected and gave Hitler the crucial votes he needed for emergency powers."—"No less a figure than Herman Goering, second in rank in the Nazi hierarchy, confessed that he felt overawed when ushered into his presence." [81]

Pius XII 1939-1958 Silence is Golden

"When thousands of German anti-Nazis were tortured to death in Hilter's concentration camps, when the Polish intelligentsia was slaughtered, when hundreds of thousands of Russians died as a result of being treated as Slavic unter-menschen, and when six million human beings were murdered for being 'non-Aryan' Catholic, church officials in Germany bolstered the regime perpetrating these crimes, the pope in Rome, the spiritual head and supreme moral teacher remained silent." [82]

"Did Pius carry neutrality too far in refusing to publically denounce the Nazi atrocities against the Jews, the Poles, the Serbs and others? There is no doubt the pope was fully informed about the extent and nature of these crimes and yet he kept silent." [83]

Paul VI 1963-1978 Holy Father or Godfather?

"…became a subject of scorn and derision. Stories appeared in the press that the 'Holy Father' had lost up to $1 billion because of clandestine dealings with the mafia. The Jesuits attacked the pope for his interference in Italian politics and his placement of 'The church's future in the hands of Satan.'"—"The Traditionalist," a Catholic weekly newspaper, after publishing a detailed account of the Sindona affair in February, 1973, called the pope, 'A traitor to the church.'" [84]

John Paul II 1978-2005
Lifting up the "Mother of God" to a lost and dying world

"His visits to the major shrines at Fatima and Lourdes have underscored his very strong devotion to the Blessed Mother. At Fatima in 1982 he re-consecrated the whole world to the virgin and prayed for its deliverance from hunger, sins against life, injustices and nuclear war. His encyclical 'Mater Redemptoris' (March 25, 1987) a comprehensive scriptural, conciliar, and theological meditation of the 'Mother of God' to all Christians, calling on them to accept her as the source of unity because she is their 'common Mother', has attained worldwide recognition as 'Mater Redemptoris' of the whole world." [85]

And Mary said: my soul glorifies the Lord and my spirit rejoices in God my savior.

Luke 1:47

No More Deception

We do not use deception, nor do we distort the word of God. On the contrary, by setting forth the truth plainly we commend ourselves to every man's conscience in the sight of God.

II Corinthians 4:2

Do you not know that the wicked will not inherit the kingdom of God? Do not be deceived.

II Corinthians 6:9

See to it that no one takes you captive through hollow and deceptive philosophy, which depends on human tradition and the basic principles of this world rather than on Christ.

Colossians 2:8

As bad and as evil as some of the scoundrels were, committing sins of fornication, adultery, murder, theft, greed, and violence, not one of them tried to eliminate one of the commandments.[86]

"By virtue of his office, the Roman pontiff possesses infallibility in teaching when as the supreme pastor and teacher of all Christians he proclaims by definitive act that a doctrine of faith and morals is to be held."—"All the faithful must believe that the Apostolic See and the Roman pontiff hold primacy over the whole world." [87]

"He has the last and final word. There is no appeal above the pope's authority since he is considered the Vicar of Christ on earth."[88]

A Moral Dilemma

Rome's long line of evil and immoral popes have created a real moral dilemma for the Catholic Church. How can a church that claims to be the supreme pastor and moral teacher of all Christians insist that her 'faithful' obey the moral teaching of her evil and immoral popes?

According to the Catholic Church the answer to that perplexing moral absurdity can be provided by her immoral popes. It was Christ who appointed them supreme pastors and moral teachers over the whole world when he told Peter: "And I tell you that you are Peter, and on this rock I will build my church." (Matthew 16:18) The fact that He (Christ) is the rock that he was referring to is irrelevant to Rome.

The important thing to remember according to the Catholic Church is this; when Christ spoke these words he placed all who would believe in Him and His all sufficient and finished work of the cross under the sovereign control of the Roman pontiffs, including the evil and immoral ones! Incredible!

3

The Misplaced Faith of Millions

The Gospel of Jesus
The Gospel Paul Preached

For it is by grace you have been saved, through faith and this not from yourselves, it is the gift of God—not by works, so that no one can boast."

Ephesians 2:8.9

This righteousness from God comes through faith in Jesus Christ to all who believe."

Romans 3:22

For we maintain that a man is justified by faith apart from observing the law."

Romans 3:28

The Gospel of Rome
The Legalistic Gospel of Sacramental Grace

In a never ending effort to ensure legalistic obedience to the papacy, Rome would add to her perverted gospel of sacramental grace 2,414 ecclesiastical laws, these she would codify in the "Codex Iuris Canonici." [89]

No longer would a personal faith in Christ and the cross be sufficient for salvation. The sacraments, not faith would become the primary vehicle through which god conveys grace.

Sacramental Grace

The Catholic gospel of sacramental grace does not confer God's amazing grace on mankind but Rome's maze of grace. According to Catholicism, Christ instituted seven rituals or sacraments. The sacraments were given exclusively to the church by Christ for the purpose of conferring God's grace in its various forms on mankind. The faithful become members in good standing of the one true church of Christ, if they undergo an initiation.

There are three sacraments or church rituals to be received by the faithful whereby their relationship and connection to the church (not Christ) is fully established—Baptism, confirmation, and Holy Eucharist.

"They are called the sacraments of initiation." [90]

"The sacraments are the primary vehicle through which God conveys grace. Sacramental grace is the grace conferred by the valid and fruitful reception of the sacraments." [91]

Rome's Maze of Grace

"Christ bestowed on the church of Rome and her 'most holy fathers' exclusive authority to confer the following categories of God's grace on 'the faithful': Sacramental, actual, efficacious, gratuitous, habitual, justifying, sanating, sanctifying, sufficient, elevating, baptismal, interior, illuminating, uncreated and preventing!" [92]

"Sanctifying grace makes a person holy by the indwelling of the trinity, it is essentially obtained by baptism, it can be increased through good works but you lose it through mortal sin." [93]

On the other hand, "actual grace is supernatural help from God." [94]

I will have mercy on whom I have mercy, and I will have compassion on whom I have compassion.

Exodus 33:19, Romans 9:15

God's grace is not conferred on sinful men through rituals performed by sinful men. The sacraments have no more power to confer God's grace than a Band-Aid has to cure cancer!

It is by grace you have been saved through faith and this not from yourselves, it is the gift of God.

Ephesians 2:8

For all have sinned and fall short of the glory of God and are justified freely by his grace through the redemption that came by Christ Jesus. God presented him as a sacrifice of atonement, through faith in his blood.

Romans 3:23,25

The gospel of sacramental grace clearly perverts the gospel of Christ, it was never taught or practiced by the apostles. It originated in the minds of sinful men who abandoned their faith in Christ and his finished and all sufficient sacrifice of the cross, 'scoundrels' and 'knaves' who "neglected to guide the chariot of the bride of the crucified along the path so clearly marked for her."

Water Baptism

The Catholic Church teaches that fallen humanity needs sanctifying grace (supernatural divine assistance) and that God has bestowed on the church of Rome the exclusive power and authority to confer this grace on fallen humanity. "Only baptism confers this special grace; without this grace the soul cannot enter heaven." [95]

Infant Baptism

"Regarding the limbo of infants, it is an article of faith that those who die without baptism, and for whom the want of baptism has not been supplied in some other way, cannot enter heaven, this is the teaching of the ecumenical councils of Florence and Trent." [96]

"The only remedy for original sin and its effects is divine grace. The grace of baptism is sanctifying grace. It washes away original sin and restores the broken relationship between the created man and the creator." [97]

The Convoluted Smoke and Mirrors Theology of Roman Catholicism

"If you hold to my teaching, you are really my disciples, then you will know the truth, and the truth will set you free."

John 8:31,32

On the one hand, the Catholic Church insists that her so called 'bad popes' were never really qualified to be valid ministers of the gospel.

"The Roman Catholic Church has always insisted that for a valid ministry...apostolic succession is not simply identifed with the historical chain of bishops but depends also on fidelity to the gospel and conformity of life and word to the teaching of the apostles."[98] (emphasis added)

On the other hand, as the successors of Peter, "all the faithful must believe that the Apostolic See and the Roman pontiff hold primacy over the whole world." [All the successors of Peter] "are the true vicars of Christ, the head of the whole church and faith, and teacher of all Christians."[99]

The Church of Rome, it would appear, formulates her theology on one basic principle, if we can convince the 'faithful' to check their God-given brains at the door of the Magesterium, we can tell them anything and they will believe it!

Anonymous Catholics

(**Unlike unbaptized infants**), God does not punish "Anonymous Catholics:" "Anyone through no fault of his own [who] has not consciously or willingly rejected Christ and His church is not culpable (guilty), and God does not punish us for things for which we are not responsible." [100]

"...God fearing Jews, Muslims, Hindus, Taoists, Buddhists, and those of all faiths who do not know Christ and his *Catholic Church* are necessary for salvation, and as a result have not deliberately rejected Christ, are not penalized for what they do not know."(emphasis added) [101]

"...If a person follows his or her religion to the best of their ability according to the rules of their religion, then it is believed that he intuitively desired baptism."—"It would be unfair and unjust for a person who does not have the gift of faith in Jesus to be denied heaven." [102] (With one notable exception, infants who die without baptism!)

I tell you the truth, no one can enter into God's kingdom without being born of water and spirit.

John 3:5

John 3:5 is Rome's scriptural source for her doctrine regarding the necessity of water baptism. The fact that John 3:5 has absolutely nothing to do with water baptism is irrelevant (at least to Rome).

Nicodemus had just asked Jesus: "How can a man be born when he is old? Surely he cannot enter a second time into his mother's womb to be born." (John 3:4) Nicodemus is asking Jesus, how can there be two natural births? Jesus responds by telling him there is only one natural birth, which he refers to as being "born of water,"

Water: the [amniotic] fluid surrounding the fetus in the uterus. [103]

He then tells Nicodemus there is a spiritual rebirth. He clarifies his meaning in verse six, "flesh gives birth to flesh but the Spirit gives birth to Spirit." What further complicates Rome's insistence that water baptism is necessary for salvation: "I am thankful I did not baptize any of you…for Christ did not send me to baptize but to preach the Gospel." I Corinthians 1:14, 17

Repentance

Water baptism does not confer anything, it symbolizes the death of the sinful nature and the resurrection of a new life in Christ Jesus:

Water symbolizes baptism that now saves you also—not the removal of dirt from the body but the pledge of a good conscience toward God.

I Peter 3:21

John the Baptist's water baptism was not a baptism that conferred a special grace necessary for salvation: "I baptize you with water for repentance."

Matthew 3:11

John's baptism was a baptism of repentance.

Acts 19:4

Produce fruit in keeping with repentance.

Matthew 3:8

From that time on Jesus began to preach, 'repent for the kingdom of God is near.

Matthew 4:17

Repentance is not penance

No church or religious institution can grant or confer repentance. Repentance is not to be confused with penance. Repentance is characterized by a heart-felt desire to turn from sin and turn to God with faith in Christ and His finished work of the cross, trusting that He has paid the full price for all punishment due.

According to Rome, penance is punishment: "A sacrament instituted by Christ in the form of judgment for the remission of sin done after baptism." [104]

Penance is imposed by the Church of Rome as punishment for sin, it takes salvation out of God's hands and places it squarely in the hands of the Catholic Church.

God's kindness leads you toward repentance.

Romans 2:4

Repentance leads sinful man to faith in the finished work of the cross, where:

"There is now no condemnation for those who are in Christ Jesus."

Romans 8:1

"I will have mercy on whom I will have mercy and I will have compassion on whom I will have compassion."

Exodus 33:19; Romans 9:15

The Church of Rome's divine revelation on who gets into heaven and who does not: Unbaptized infants are out! God fearing Jews, Muslims, Hindus, Taoists and Buddhists, are in! Those who do not have the gift of faith in Jesus are in! Those who do not know that the Catholic Church is necessary for salvation are in! Those who know that the Catholic Church is not necessary for salvation, definitely out!

The Eucharistic Sacrifice of the Mass

Nothing declares the futility of fallen humanity to achieve salvation apart from the cross and exposes his delusions of self righteousness more than the grandiose notion that God is pleased when a self anointed royal priesthood of sinners turns bread and wine into the appearance of Jesus and offers him in sacrifice!

Transubstantiation:
The Magic of the Magesterium

Keep on with your magic spells and with your many sorceries."

Isaiah 47:12

By your magic spell all the nations were led astray.

Revelation 18:23

"Through the words the priest uses at the consecration, 'this is my body...this is my blood,' Christ is made present. Bread and wine cease to exist, and they become the body and blood of Christ; this doctrine is called transubstantiation." [105]

"While the faith behind this term was already believed in apostolic times, the term itself was a later development." [106]

Transubstantiation was never believed in, or taught by the apostles. What the apostles believed is exactly what Jesus intended:

*This is my body given for you, **do this in remembrance of me.***
(emphasis added)

Luke 22:19

*For I received from the Lord what I also passed onto you: the Lord Jesus, on the night he was betrayed took bread and when he had given thanks, he broke it and said, 'This is my body, which is for you, **do this in remembrance of me**,' in the same way, after supper he took the cup, saying 'This cup is the new covenant in my blood, do this whenever you drink it, **in remembrance of me**.'"* (emphasis added)

I Corinthians 11:23-25

Apparently when Paul wrote to the church at Corinth to tell them what he had received from the Lord regarding the last supper he neglected to mention that God had given him the power and authority to bring his son down from heaven, make him appear in the form of bread and wine, and offer him in sacrifice!

"Originally called the Lord's supper, it was a simple service consisting of prayers by the whole assembly followed by a kiss of peace." [107]

"As late as the fifth century, John Chrysostom still stressed preaching as the main task of the Christian minister. The more elaborate liturgy of the post Constantinian era, with its features borrowed from paganism, enhanced the image of the minister as a sacred personage." [108](emphasis added)

"The transcendental, awesome, and mysterious nature of the mass was allowed to blot out almost completely the original spirit of community participation, it was something that happened at the altar, it was the epiphany of God. It was something you watched. The various actions of the priest were no longer intelligible in this context, so they were given mystical and allegorical significance."—"Sometimes they would pay the priest a special stipend just to hold the host up higher and for a longer time." [109]

"It was at the mass that the separation of clergy from people was made dramatically evident. While the mass had retained its basic meal structure, even in the early centuries it began to move away from its original character as a action of the whole community."—"The mass became exclusively the priests business, with the people reduced to the role of spectators." [110]

This is what is written: The Christ will suffer and rise from the dead on the third day, and repentance and forgiveness of sins will be preached in His name to all nations.

Luke 24: 46,47

"As with the Curia and the higher clergy, we find every grade of decay: the so called mass priests, who constituted in many cities as much as 10 percent of the population: their only function was to say daily mass, preaching seems to have been on a very low level." [111]

For if someone comes to you and preaches a Jesus other than the Jesus we preached, or if you receive a different gospel from the one you accepted, you put up with it easily enough.

II Corinthians 11:4

The Jesus of the Mass is Another Jesus

Catholicism's Jesus of the mass is not the Jesus of the bible. He awaits the beckoning call of a royal priesthood comprised of sinful men, ("Knaves and Scoundrel"), who can make him continually and mystically appear under the appearance of bread and wine. He appears and is ingested by the "Faithful," which in turn produces a warm and fuzzy feeling of being partakers, sharers, and participants in his act. The Jesus of the mass perpetuates his atoning sacrifice at every mass through the mystical words of the priest; "

"Jesus is priest and victim at every mass (He is the one offering and being offered) and uses the priesthood to perpetuate his holy sacrifice. Through the words the priest uses at the consecration, "This is my body. This is my blood." Christ is made present. The re-presentation means that because Christ is really present he is capable now as he was on Good Friday of freely offering himself to the Father." [112]

"The same Christ who offered himself once in a bloody manner on the altar of the cross, is present and offered in an unbloody manner, Consequently, the mass is a truly propitiatory sacrifice, which means that by this oblation the Lord is appeased." [113]

"The Holy Sacrifice of the mass , is not a second or other sacrifice, it is one and the same sacrifice of the cross re-enacted in an unbloody fashion." [114]

"This bread on which I gaze, this bread now on high it is you yourself, your very flesh; this I believe and trust."—"Truly do I believe that this blood now offered in the chalice is your own, once given to the Father, truly the same that gushed forth 'neath scourge and lance, most truly the blood that flows forever from your wounds." [115]

"For it is we ourselves who offer to the Father this lamb who now mystically sacrifices himself; we are partakers, sharers, participants in his act." [116]

The Jesus of the Mass

The Jesus of the mass is literally worshiped as bread and wine. [117]

"When the priest pronounces his tremendous words of consecration, he reaches up into heaven, brings Christ down from His throne, and places Him upon our altar to be offered up again as the victim for the sins of man. It is a power greater than that of monarchs and emperors: It is greater than that of saints and angels, greater than that of Seraphim and Cherubim." [118]

"Indeed it is greater even than the power of the Virgin Mary. While the blessed virgin was the human agency by which Christ became incarnate a single time, the priest brings Christ down from heaven and renders Him present on our altar as the eternal victim for the sins of man—not once but a thousand times! *The priest speaks and lo! Christ, the eternal and omnipotent God, bows his head in humble obedience to the priest's command* (emphasis added)." [119]

The spirit clearly says that in later times some will abandon the faith and follow deceiving spirits and things taught by demons.

I Timothy 4:1

The Real Jesus: The Jesus of the Bible

Such a high priest meets our need—one who is holy, blameless, pure, set apart from sinners, exalted above the heavens, Unlike the other high priests, he does not need to offer sacrifices day after day, first for his own sins, and then for the sins of the people. He sacrificed for their sins once for all when he offered himself.

Hebrews 7:26, 27

But now he has appeared once for all at the end of the ages to do away with sin by the sacrifice of himself. Just as man is destined to die once, and after that to face judgment, so Christ was sacrificed once to take away the sins of many people; He will appear a second time, not to bear sin, but to bring salvation to those who are waiting for him.

Hebrews 9:26-28

When the real Jesus appears to man he does not appear as bread or wine, which in turn produces a warm and fuzzy feeling of being "partakers," "sharers," and "participants" in his "act." When the Jesus of the Bible appears to man, he appears in His glory, which in turn produces shock and awe! (Matthew 24:30; Acts 9:3-6; Philippians 2:9-11; Revelation 1:12-17)

The Real Jesus Sacrificed Once for all.

We have been made holy through the sacrifice of the body of Jesus Christ once for all. Day after day every priest stands and performs his religious duties; again and again he offers the same sacrifices; which can never take away sins. But when this priest had offered for all time one sacrifice for sins, he sat down at the right hand of God. Since that time he waits for his enemies to be made his footstool, because by one sacrifice he has made perfect forever those who are being made holy."

Hebrews 10:10-14

The real Jesus of the Bible knows that without his shedding of blood there can be no forgiveness of sin. (Hebrews 9:22)

The real Jesus is not worshipped as bread and wine but in spirit and truth. (John 4:23)

The last words of the real Jesus of the Bible before giving up his spirit on the cross: "It is finished." (John 18:30)

He appeared once for all at the end of the age to do away with sin by the sacrifice of Himself.

Hebrews 9:26

The real Jesus does not depend on sinful man to gradually and continually confer God's grace on sinful mankind through the sacrifice of the mass.

It does not, therefore, depend on man's desire or effort, but on God's mercy.

Romans 9:16

For Christ died for sins once for all.

I Peter 3:18

The Bread of Life

Whenever Jesus referred to himself as bread, he was speaking figuratively. Bread as food nourishes our physical bodies, Christ (and his all sufficient and finished work of the cross) is the real bread that nourishes the soul. He removes the sting of death caused by sin, and through faith grants eternal life to all who believe.

Christ always pointed to the redemptive power of his one and only bloody sacrifice for the sins of a lost and dying world. Because a merciful and Holy God has by one sacrifice made perfect forever those who are being made holy, there is no need for sinful man to continually offer Christ in the form of bread to His Father. In order to justify her cannibalistic doctrine of transubstantiation she must abandon her own principles of interpreting any text in the context of what came before and after that passage. If Jesus was not teaching that he was to be turned into bread and ingested by the faithful, her man-made perverted gospel will collapse like a house of cards!

I tell you the truth, he who believes has everlasting life, I am the bread of life, your forefathers ate the manna in the dessert, yet they died. But here is the bread that comes down from heaven, which a man may eat and not die. I am the living bread that came down from heaven, if anyone eats of this bread, he will live forever. ***This bread is my flesh, which I will give for the life of the world.*** *(emphasis added)*

John 6:47-51

When Jesus states: "He who believes has everlasting life," he is clearly not referring to changing into the appearance of bread to be consumed and offered in sacrifice He is referring to exactly what he makes so abundantly clear in verse 51: "This bread is my flesh, which I will give for the life of the world."—He is obviously referring to His one all-sufficient and bloody sacrifice on the cross.

This is the bread that came down from heaven (not a wafer),
your forefathers ate manna and died, but he who feeds on this
bread (faith in His one and all sufficient bloody sacrifice),
will live forever.

John 6:58

The spirit gives life; the flesh counts for nothing, The words I
have spoken to you are spirit and they are life.

John 6:63

Jesus makes it abundantly clear he is not a baked food we eat in order to nourish and sustain our perishable bodies. He is the spiritual sustenance that nourishes and sustains our souls unto eternal life, and all who trust in Him and His atoning sacrifice will never perish.

Look the Lamb of God, who takes away the sin of the world.

John 1:29 (Jesus is not a young sheep)

I am the true vine.

John 15:1 (Jesus is not a plant)

I am the good shepherd.

John 10:24 (Jesus is not a sheep herder)

I am the gate for the sheep.

John 10: 7, 9 (Jesus is not a swinging, movable structure)

I am the bread of life.

John 6:35 (Jesus is not a baked food made of flour)

The Eucharistic Jesus of the mass who is routinely sacrificed to God in the form of bread and wine and eaten by the faithful bears a striking resemblance to the gods of ancient pagans who routinely offered sacrifices to their gods and would actually eat part of the cooked flesh of the sacrifice. They would have considered eating the sacrificed flesh as becoming one with god—sharing an identity with that deity.

Therefore God exalted him to the highest place and gave Him the name that is above every name, that at the name of Jesus every knee should bow, in heaven and on earth and under the earth, and every tongue confess that Jesus Christ is Lord, to the glory of God the Father.

Philippians 2:9-11

This same Jesus, who has been taken from you into heaven will come back in the same way you have seen him go into heaven.

Acts 1:11

The author of Acts got it wrong. Jesus makes regular appearances, just not in the same way the apostles saw him go into heaven!

Destination Purgatory

While we wait for the blessed hope the appearing of our great God and savior, Jesus Christ, who gave himself for us to redeem us from all wickedness and to purify for himself a people that are his very own.

Titus 2:14

Purgatory

"The place or condition in which the souls of the just are purified after death and before they can enter heaven." [120]

"A place or condition of expiation (atonement), suffering or remorse." [121]

"The sufferings in purgatory are not the same for all, but proportioned to each person's degree of sinfulness, moreover, their sufferings can be lessened in duration and intensity through the prayers and good works of the faithful on earth." 'As members of the church suffering' the souls in purgatory can intercede for the persons on earth, who are therefore encouraged to invoke their aid." [122]

Only God knows how this "doctrine of demons" wormed its way into the Roman playbook. Not only does it deny the all sufficient sacrifice of the cross, but it places atonement for sin in the hands of the faithful on earth, the souls in purgatory, and of course, the Church of Rome.

The purpose of this "sacred doctrine" appears to be three fold:

1. Encourage the faithful on earth to pray for, and do good works for the souls in the holding tank of purgatory, so they will get out as soon as possible.

2. Encourage the souls in the holding tank of purgatory to intercede for the faithful on earth before they depart and go to the holding tank

3. Make sure the holding tank is always filled to capacity to ensure uninterrupted revenue for Rome through the sale of indulgences

Bad News for the Faithful

Catholics are not likely to enter heaven until they spend time suffering for their sins in purgatory. From Peter to Pius X there have been 258 pontiffs, this number comprises only sixty saints. [123]

If it is hard for her "most holy fathers" to get into heaven, it is not likely "the faithful" will be spared the punishment of purgatory. As to whether or not the sacred doctrine regarding purgatory was divinely revealed to the magisterium[124] through sacred scripture or sacred tradition, is not clear, one thing we do know, it has made a fortune for Rome through the sale of indulgences.

Indulgence

"The remission before God of the temporal punishment due to sins forgiven, as far as their guilt is concerned."—"Which the follower of Christ with the proper dispositions and under certain determined conditions acquires through the intervention of the church." [125]

Tetzel
(Rome's Traveling Salesman)

"It was the arrival in the German town of Wittenburg of the Dominican priest Johann Tetzel in October 1517 that sparked the first Lutheran revolt. Tetzel was to all intents and purposes a traveling salesman. His boss, Pope Leo X (1531) had devised a new sales campaign to get funds for refurbishing St. Peter's Basilica in Rome. His wares: indulgences, his prices: exact monetary value for the forgiveness of every imaginable sin of the already dead. His sales technique: a cardinal red booth, a receipt box, and a marvelous gift for mimicking the pleas of the dead who suffered in purgatory and craved the monetary help of the living so that they might escape the punishment of eternal fire, his sales pitch: a memorable jingle: 'As soon as the coin in the coffer rings, the soul from purgatory springs.'" [126]

A Royal Sham

"The remission of punishment for sins forgiven." Incredible! Why would a Holy and righteous God inflict punishment on mankind for sins He has forgiven through the atoning sacrifice of His Son?

If you belong to a church that teaches, after death the soul goes to a place of punishment called purgatory, but you can get out early through an indulgence granted by the church in exchange for some good work (often a donation of money), I implore you to do a couple of things. First, prayerfully read Isaiah 53:5, 6 and second, head for the exit!

He was pierced for our transgressions,

He was crushed for our iniquities;

The punishment that brought us peace was upon him,

And by his wounds we are healed.

We all like sheep have gone astray,

Each of us has turned to his own way:

And the Lord has laid on him

The iniquity of us all.

Isaiah 53; 5,6

4

The Mother of God

The deification and worship of Mary is just another example of why theological honesty, integrity, and sincerity have never been, nor ever will be, the hallmarks of Roman Catholicism. The fact that there is no scripture or apostolic tradition to support such an abomination is irrelevant; "*It was the Catholic Church that was commissioned by Christ to teach all nations and to teach them infallibly. The mere fact that the church teaches the doctrine is a guarantee that it is true.*"—"*Let it just be said that if the position of the Catholic Church is true, then the notion of Sola Scriptura is false.* There is then no problem with the church officially defining a doctrine which, though not in contradiction to scripture, cannot be found on its face."(emphasis added) [127]

If you are a member of the church that claims exclusive 'God-given' authority to condemn you to hell for rejecting any of her 'God-given' precepts, you can take comfort in knowing how her doctrines came into existence: sinful popes spoke, and presto! the abominable doctrines had to be accepted as true. This is precisely how Mary evolved from the humble biological mother of Jesus into the exalted 'Mother of God,' 'Queen of Heaven,' 'Queen of the Universe,' 'Immaculate Mother,' 'Mediatrix,' and 'Coredemptrix.' Even if Jesus had referred to Mary as the greatest person ever born (that privilege belonged to John the Baptist—Matthew 11:11), no created being is worthy of that which belongs to the creator.

If you buy into Catholicism's specious "hyperdouleia"[128] argument (the worship of Mary is a notch below that which is offered to her creator), you can probably be sold on the notion that Christ bows His head in humble submission when the priest offers Him in sacrifice!

"Hyperdouleia, [which] is the enhanced exclusive worship of Mary, Interestingly, the word douleia in the New Testament is always used for slavery, bondage, or subservience." [129]

Men, why are you doing this?

Acts 14:15

While preaching the gospel in the city of Lystra, the crowds tried to deify Barnabas and Paul after observing the miracles God had performed through them. Their response: A resounding, "Men, why are you doing this?" No true servant of Jesus Christ would accept 'hyperdouleia' or any form of self glorification. Mary's response to hearing that she had been elevated by the Church of Rome to the divine status of 'Mother of God,' would have been identical to that of Barnabas and Paul. The serpents tactics have not changed, by making the created Mary the Immaculate Mother of her creator, the saved servant becomes worthy of the adoration and devotion due her creator and savior.

The Great Mother Goddess

The ancient religions of the world always had their great mother goddess, in Rome she was identified as Maia, Ops, Teilus and Ceres.[130] Now that Christianity had become the official religion of Rome, what better way to appease her new master than to provide him with her very own version of the great mother goddess.

"At first the virgin was not honored above other saints, but from the fourth century onwards there was a marked growth in the devotion accorded by Christians to Mary. In 431 the Council of Ephesus, which met in a church supposed to contain her mortal remains, confirmed the title of 'Theotokos,' 'God-bearer' which was translated into Latin as 'mater dei,' "Mother of God." In 1950 Pope Pius XII proclaimed by the bull munificentissimus deus, the dogma of the bodily ascent into heaven of the virgin Mary."—"In the eastern church the popularity of her cult is evident in the plethora of icons and sacred images." [131]

"Catholics might be surprised how late was this proliferation of Marian titles and feasts. There were no church celebrations of her, at least in the west, till well past the fifth century. In all the hundreds of Augustine's sermons, there is not one preached about her." [132]

Thomas Aquinas (Thirteenth Century)

"Argued forcefully against the immaculate conception of Mary. All humans descended from Adam, he maintained, inherit the blight of original sin. To exempt Mary from this human condition would mean that Jesus was not born a man in the line of David, taking on himself the human condition of sin he meant to defeat… The early doctrines of Marian glory clarified the character of the incarnation and were centered on Mary's son. This doctrine would muddy and confuse the nature of the incarnation. Exemption from the historical human condition would make Mary superhuman." [133]

It took several hundred years of divine revelation and countless Marian apparitions before the successors of Peter finally realized that Jesus and his apostles inadvertently neglected to lay the foundation for the sound doctrine regarding the veneration, adoration, and worship of "God's mother."

Jesus respected his mother but he accorded her no special honor.

As Jesus was saying these things, a woman in the crowd called out, 'Blessed is the mother who gave you birth and nursed you.' He replied, 'blessed rather are those who hear the word of God and obey it.'

Luke 11:27, 28 (See also Matthew 12:46-50

The Immaculate Conception

"The doctrine of the immaculate conception of Mary teaches that she was preserved from original sin from the first moment of her conception in the womb of St. Ann. By a special privilege of grace Mary was preserved from all venial sin and in fact she was impeccable."—"It was always believed as an article of faith by the church." [134]

In 1854, Pius IX (The mentally ill pope)[135] declared by the bull 'ineffabilis deus' that Mary was sinless from her first moment of conception, he further declared that it was 'a doctrine revealed by God' and therefore must be believed firmly and constantly by all the faithful. [136]

The same pope who declared Mary sinless also declared himself infallible. Church revisionists have been scrambling ever since this megalomaniac proclaimed: "I am tradition, I am the church." [137]

"Neither the Greek nor Latin fathers explicitly taught the immaculate conception." [138]

"The Franciscans in the fourteenth century promoted the idea that Mary was immaculately conceived in that her son never bore the stain of original sin." [139]

"The immaculate conception had to be clarified before becoming explicit dogma, main credit for this goes to Franciscan John Duns Scotus (1264-1308). [140]

Aquinas and Augustine

If you disagree with Pius IX's papal decree on the immaculate conception you are excommunicated and condemned to hell! But take heart, so are two of her most venerable theologians!

Pius IX infallibly declared that you are excommunicated and dammed to hell if you even think to question his divine revelation regarding the immaculate conception.

"Hence, if anyone shall dare which God forbid to think otherwise than has been defined by us, let him know and understand that he is condemned by his own judgment, that he has suffered shipwreck in the faith, that he has separated from the unity of the church and that further more by his own action he incurs the penalties established by law if he should dare to express in words or writing or by any other outward means the error he thinks in his heart." [141]

"Therefore the blessed virgin was not sanctified before her birth from the womb" and he also cites Augustine, "The sanctification, by which we become temples of God, is only of those who are born again, But no one is born again, who was not born previously, Therefore the blessed virgin was not sanctified before her birth from the womb." (Aquinas) [142]

The Immaculate Deception

Immaculate conception is an attribute of divinity which belongs only to the incarnate word of God, Jesus Christ;

The Word became flesh and made His dwelling among us. We have seen his glory, the glory of the one and only, who came from the Father, full of grace and truth.

John 1:14

By proclaiming Mary, (the humble servant) the sinless mother of God, Rome has firmly established in the minds of her 'faithful' that she is worthy of special veneration and devotion. The 'Queen of Heaven,' 'Queen of the Universe,' 'Mediatrix,' and 'Co-Redemtrix,' now deserves our 'hyperdouleia,' (another term 'Holy Mother' has stored in her theological lexicon of smoke and mirrors). The immaculate conception and assumption of Mary are infallibly declared dogma, "The source of infallibility is the supernatural assistance of the Holy Spirit, who protects the supreme teacher (the pope) of the church from error." [143]

Apparently, the Holy Spirit must provide this protection to all of Peter's successors, even though they may be 'scoundrels' and 'knaves', supreme teachers who engaged in murder, theft, adultery, and fornication. "This protection from the 'Holy Spirit' ensures that 'the people of God' are not mislead by their supreme teacher." [144] Incredible!

The immaculate conception and the assumption of Mary are found no where in scripture, and there was never any apostolic tradition regarding the veneration due her as the 'Mother of God.' The apostles make no mention of her in their letters to the churches.

Paul, the apostle called by God to preach and teach the Gospel that he received by divine revelation from Jesus, not only neglects to mention Mary, but specifically refutes the Church of Rome's doctrine of the Immaculate Conception:

There is no one righteous, not even one.

Romans 3:10

For all have sinned and fall short of the glory of God.

Romans 3:23

Therefore, just as sin entered the world through one man, and death through sin, in this way death came to all men, because all sinned.

Romans 5:12

Just as the result of one trespass was condemnation for all men, so also the result of one act of righteousness was justification that brings life for all men.

Romans 5:18

The Great Assumption of Pius XII

Like the Immaculate Conception, there is no sacred scripture or apostolic tradition to support Mary's bodily ascent into heaven. Therefore 'the faithful' must assume that it was divinely revealed to the Church of Rome, or more specifically to Pius XII in 1950.

One can't help but wonder why Pius did not receive some divine revelation in 1940 regarding the gross immorality of bolstering a regime that put six million human beings to death for being non-Aryan. Why was there no divine revelation in the face of the greatest of moral depravities which mankind has been forced to witness in recent centuries? The moral teachings of a church and her sovereign pontiff, dedicated to love and charity, could be heard in no other form but vague generalities.

Theologically Sound Doctrine, or More Theological Smoke and Mirrors?

"While there is no direct evidence of the assumption in the Bible, implicitly the church argues from Mary's fullness of grace (Luke 1:28) "the church does not rely on the scriptures for belief in Mary's assumption. In explaining the grounds for the church's belief, Pius XII singled out the fact that Mary was the "Mother of God." [145]

"Pius XII solemnly defined Mary's assumption for all generations. In this document the pope states that because Mary did not have original sin due to her immaculate conception, she did not have to suffer decay on earth, instead, her divine son Jesus assumed her body and soul into heaven." [146]

"In the past 150 years, there have been only two dogmas regarding this issue that have been formally defined by the pope in an excathedra statement of papal infallibility. The first is the dogma of immaculate conception of Mary in 1854, and the second is the dogma of the assumption of Mary in 1950." [147]

Once the 'faithful' assume the immaculate conception and the bodily assumption of Mary are divinely revealed truths and official dogma of the church of Rome, they can also assume that they are going to spend a lot of time in purgatory or quite possibly lose the salvation won for them by Christ at the cross if they reject the church's teaching that Mary was sinless and assumed bodily into heaven; 'Catholic Dogma': "It is to be believed by all the faithful as part of divine revelation—moreover, their acceptance by the faithful must be proposed as necessary for salvation." [148]

How Mary Became "The Mother of God" "Theotokos" [149]

Nestorius, the bishop of Constantinople, believed that in Jesus Christ were two persons joined together, namely, God the Son (the Word) and the man Jesus. Jesus was the dwelling place of the word, he alone was born of Mary. The Catholic teaching was that from its first moment Christ's human nature existed as the human nature of the word and never as a single, independently existing nature: God and man is one Christ, one person in two natures.

In support of the orthodox belief that Christ was a divine person who assumed a human nature, the majority at the Council of Ephesus (431) felt it appropriate to apply to Mary the word 'Theotokos,' 'God Bearer,' 'Mother of God.'

The council's purpose in applying the term 'Theotokos' to Mary was not to glorify Mary or assign to her a divine attribute, it was meant to support their belief that Christ was a divine person who assumed a human nature.

A Theological Progression of Smoke and Mirrors

In 431 the Council of Ephesus (in order to support the belief that Christ was a divine person who assumed a human nature) felt that it would be appropriate to apply the word 'God bearer' to Mary. 1400 years later God revealed to Pius IX that if Mary was the 'Mother of God' she would have to be sinless. Ninety-six years later God revealed to Pius XII that if God revealed to Pius IX that Mary was the sinless 'Mother of God,' she would have to be assumed bodily into heaven.

Share the Glory

All this 'divine revelation' has served but one purpose to a lost and dying world: Christ, our Lord and Savior, the incarnate Word, can now share His glory with the 'Queen of the Universe'!

"When the mother of Jesus does come up in the gospel passages," Augustine expounds, "he does not find the deep importance of her role that modern preachers do. In the gospel of John, for instance, Jesus looks down from the cross at Mary and Saint John, telling them, 'Mother, this is your son, and son, this is your mother' (John 19:27). I have heard many Lenten sermons that claim we are all, along with John, given into Mary's care as our protectress, making her a symbol of the church. But Augustine looks at the gospels next words, 'From that moment John took her to his own,' and makes the obvious conclusion that she is committed to John's care. Augustine even says that Jesus is reminding his disciples of their duty to care for the old and widowed." [150]

The Mediatrix of All Graces

"Ad Diem Illum"—"Encyclical of Pope Pius X, 1904, explaining that Mary is the mediatrix of all graces—the principal agent in distributing graces." [151]

For there is one God and one mediator between God and men,
the man Christ Jesus.

I Timothy 2:5

"Mediatrix"

"A title of the blessed virgin as mediator of grace'—Mary freely co-operated with God in consenting to the incarnation, giving birth to her son and thus sharing with him in spirit the labors of his passion and death." [152]

"Mary co-operates by material intercession in applying Christ's redemptive grace to human beings—according to God's special ordinance, the graces merited by Christ conferred through the actual intercessory mediation of his mother." [153]

"As mother of the redeemer and saint in heaven, she is a powerful advocate and intercessor for us on earth." [154]

Jesus did not consider his biological mother the 'Mother of God.' (Matthew 12:46-50) Mary did not consider herself sinless. (Luke 1:46, 47)

Paul explicitly refutes Rome's dogma that declares Mary was born without sin. (Romans 3:10, 23; 5:12)

"Adoration of the Blessed Virgin Absolutely Forbidden" [155]

(Special veneration and devotion [Hyperdouleia] permitted!)

"Hail Holy Queen, our life, our sweetness, and our hope, to thee do we send up our sighs, mourning and weeping in this valley of tears—turn then most gracious advocate thine eyes of mercy toward us." [156]

"O most beautiful flower of Mount Carmel, fruitful vine, splendor of heaven, blessed Mother of the Son of God, immaculate virgin, assist me in this my necessity, O star of the sea, help me and show me herein you are my mother. O Holy Mary, Mother of God, Queen of heaven and earth, I humbly beseech you from the bottom of my heart to succor me in this necessity; there are none that can withstand your power." [157]

Prayer of Pope Pius XII

"Enraptured by the splendor of your heavenly beauty, and impelled by the anxieties of the world, we cast ourselves into your arms, O immaculate Mother of Jesus and our mother, Mary, confident of finding in your most loving heart appeasement of our ardent desires, and a safe harbor from the tempests which beset us on every side.

"Though degraded by our faults and overwhelmed by infinite misery, we admire and praise the peerless richness of sublime gifts with which God has filled you, above every other mere creature, from the first moment of your conception until the day on which, after your assumption into heaven, he crowned you queen of the universe. O crystal fountain of faith, bathe our minds with the eternal truths! O fragrant lily of all holiness, captivate our hearts with your heavenly perfume! O conqueress of evil and death, inspire in us a deep horror of sin, which makes the soul detestable to God and a slave of hell! O well-beloved of God, hear the ardent cry which rises up from every heart. Bend tenderly over our aching wounds. Convert the wicked, dry the tears of the afflicted and oppressed.

"Receive, O most sweet mother, our humble supplications. And above all obtain for us that, one day, happy with you, we may repeat before your throne that hymn which today is sung on earth around your altars: you are all-beautiful Mary! You are the glory, you are the joy, you are the honor of our people! Amen." [158]

You can call it veneration, you can call it adoration you can call it hyperdouleia, but please don't call it worship!

Access to Our Lord and Savior Only Through Mary

"As we have access to the Eternal Father only through Jesus Christ, so have we access to Jesus Christ only through Mary."—"By thee we have access to the son, O blessed finder of grace, bearer of life, and mother of salvation." [159]

Marian Art

"The council of Ephesus (431) ushered in a new artistic phase that began in the east but was soon introduced into Italy, Spain, and Gaul. Instead of the homely scenes from the gospel, Mary was now more often depicted as Heavenly Queen, vestured in gold and seated in royal majesty."—"Typical of the Baroque style was Mary's role as 'Conqueror of Satan' and in modern times as 'Mediatrix of Grace.'" [160]

Marianists

"Membership consists of priests and brothers, specially engaged in education on a secondary school and college level, they take the three customary vows plus a fourth vow of stability in their devotion to the blessed virgin." [161]

Mariology

"The branch of theology that studies the life and prerogatives of the blessed virgin, and her place in the economy of salvation and sanctification." [162]

Marists

"It's aim is to foster devotion to the blessed virgin." [163]

Marian Literature

"The worship of the Madonna has been one of the noblest and most vital graces." [164]

Consecration to Mary

--An act of devotion, promoted by St. Louis de Montfort

(1673—1716)

"In the presence of all the heavenly court I choose you this day for my mother and queen. I deliver and consecrate to you, as your slave, my body and soul, my goods, both interior and exterior and even the value of all my good actions, past, present, and future: leaving to you the entire and full right of disposing of me and all that belongs to me without exception, according to your good pleasure, for the greater glory of God in time and eternity, Amen." [165]

The Coronation of the Virgin

"In Florences's Uffizi Gallery, Botticelli's painting of 'The Coronation of the Virgin,' shows God wearing a papal tiara as he crowns Mary in heaven." [166]

Masquerading Angels of Light
(Shrines to the 'Mother of God')

"Mostly originate from an image which gives rise to great devotion (to Mary) and is sometimes wonder working." [167]

"The nineteenth century launched what pelican calls the age of major apparitions—no one showed more devotion to these appearances than Pope Pius IX, whom we met earlier as the kidnaper of Edgardo Mortara." [168]

For our struggle is not against flesh and blood, but against the rulers, against the authorities, against the powers of this dark world and against the spiritual forces of evil in the heavenly realms.

Ephesians 6:12

Lifting up Christ and the message of the cross to a lost and dying world

"Our lady appeared to Saint Cathrine Labourne, a nineteenth century sister of charity in Paris. She instructed this nun to create a new medal, the miraculous medal with the words, 'O Mary conceived without sin.'" [169]

"In Fatima, our lady appeared to three children—she asked for total consecration to her immaculate heart—the devotion that began was the five first Saturdays in honor of Mary Immaculate." [170]

"During the apparitions Mary told the children to have processions in honor of her immaculate conception and to tell the faithful to do penance and pray the Rosary because otherwise the world would be chastised for its sins." [171]

Prayer to the Virgin of Fatima: "Virgin of Fatima, Mother of Mercy, Queen of Heaven and earth, Refuge of Sinners, we consecrate our hearts, our souls, our families, and all we have. Furthermore we promise, O most holy virgin that we will spread devotion to you." [172]

Mary speaks to the little children at Fatima:

"You have seen hell, where the souls of poor sinners go. To save them, God wishes to establish in the world the devotion to my immaculate heart." [173]

"I want to tell you that a chapel is to be built here in my honor. I am the lady of the Rosary. Let them continue saying it every day." [174]

"In 1942 Pope Pius XII, in response to Mary's request, consecrated the world to the immaculate heart of Mary." [175]

Banneux

"The shrine of our lady of the poor, near the city of Liege in the Flemish village of Banneux. Devotion to Mary began as a result of an apparition to a poor twelve year old Belgian child in the garden of her home on June 16, 1933."—"After years of investigation, the holy see authorized public devotion to our Lady of Banneux—a statue of that title was solemnly crowned in 1956."—"Over one hundred shrines throughout the world are dedicated to our Lady of Banneux." [176]

The Message from Mary at Banneux:

"Plunge your hands into the water—this spring is reserved for me—I am the virgin of the poor."—"I come to alleviate suffering." "Believe in me I will believe in you." [177]

Our Lady of Beauraing

Belgium: "When asked if she was the immaculate virgin, she nodded her head in affirmation! When asked, what do you want? "That you always be good." She affirmed the Church of Rome's title "Immaculate Virgin," she then requested a chapel be built and stated that; "I am the Mother of God," "Queen of Heaven," pray always." [178]

Laus

"Shrine of our lady of the blessed valley. Scene of a series of apparitions in 1664 to a French shepherdess, the virgin appeared to her over a period of two months, her message: "Build a church in her honor." [179]

I am the Lord, that is my name! I will not give my glory to another.

Isaiah 42:8

Prayer to the Lady of Lourdes

"By appearing in the Grotto of Lourdes, you were pleased to make it a privileged sanctuary, whence you dispense your favors;

and already many sufferers have obtained cure of their infirmities both spiritual and corporal. I come, therefore, with the most un-bounded confidence to implore your maternal intercession. Obtain, O loving Mother, the granting of my requests. Through gratitude for favors, I will endeavor to imitate your virtues *that I may one day share your glory, Amen."* (emphasis added) [180]

"All devotions to the mother of God should lead to Jesus Christ!" (emphasis added) [181]

"Zoce," our lady of –"Marian shrine—in 1870 the Chinese were ravishing the near by country side—the little catholic group at Zoce was saved only when a sudden storm dispersed the bandits. Father Croce attributed their escape to the blessed virgin, to whom they have never ceased to pray." [182]

"Czestochowa"—"Shrine to the Black Madonna, chief Marian sanctuary of Poland—When the Turks were at the gates of Vienna, Sobieski (1624-96), the Polish King dedicated his crusade to Mary, and the west was saved. "In 1945, they came 500,000 strong to thank Mary for their liberation. In 1947 over 1,500,000 came there to beg Mary to save them from communism." [183]

"Pellevoisin" (France 1876) There were fifteen apparitions of the blessed virgin Mary to Estelle Faquette. "When Estelle prom-ised the virgin to do all she could to spread her glory, Mary replied that she should remain simple and let her actions accord with her words." [184]

Pellevoisin

"O Holy Virgin and Lady of Charity; with happiness and hu-mility I come to your feet! Virgin of miracles! You cure the sick, you give hope where there is despair, you give strength to the afflicted, preserve from disgrace our families, protect the youth, guard our children, no one can explain all the miracles and fortitude you give to the souls that come to you. We, your children, thank you for all your graces, Amen." [185]

Copacabana

"The principal Marian shrine of Bolivia—this shrine to our lady is located in the mountains near lake Titicaca. The site marked the location of an Inca temple to the sun god.—"She appeared to some Inca fisherman and led them to safety in a violent storm—in gratitude they built a small shrine in 1583.—A four-foot high statue of wood and stucco carved by descendant of Inca nobility. On feast days the Madonna is clothed in costly embroidered robes that scintillate with a thousand precious jewels—daily processions pass along the lake roads carrying a replica of their Bolivian queen of heaven as she blesses the boats off shore." [186]

"Holy Father, protect them by the power of your name, the name you gave me, while I was with them and kept them safe." John 17:11

Our Lady of Divine Love

A Roman shrine on the Via Ardeatina. "Pope Pius XII had Rome placed under special protection of our Lady of Divine Love during the war (World War II) and when hostilities ceased he declared her to have been the real savior of Rome." [187]

Saragossa

Shrine in northeastern Spain--"Mary is said to have appeared. In early Christian times, asking that a church be built in her honor." [188]

Africa

Ancient shrine at Algiers, dedicated to the Immaculate Conception. "At the shrine there are as many Muslim pilgrims as Christian, To the faithful Muslim she is "Lala Meriem" who bestows her favors." [189]

Mokameh

Shrine dedicated to the mother of divine grace—"The church is Hindu in style, and the statue of Mary is dressed in a sari with her eyes lowered in meditation. Organized groups of pilgrims, among whom are Christians, Muslims, and Hindus, arrive from great distances." [190]

Panaya Kapula

Shrine to Mary in Turkey, "Muslims as well as Christians have come here since 1691 to pay homage to Mary." [191]

The Lord almighty is the one you are to regard as holy.

Isaiah 8:13

In the United States there are six holy days—on four of them, the faithful are to regard Mary as holy: Solemnity of Mary (January 1), Assumption of the Blessed Virgin (August 15), All Saints Day (November 1; it originated in the west in 609, when Pope Boniface IV dedicated the Pantheon to the blessed virgin Mary), Mary's Immaculate Conception (December 8). [192]

How is it you are turning back to those weak and miserable principles? You are observing special days and months and seasons and years!

Galatians 4:9, 10

Holy Days of Obligation
(It's the law)

"It is not a question of choosing. Catholic Christians are expected to go to Catholic mass each and every Sunday and Holy Days of Obligation." [193]

For Satan himself masquerades as an angel of light.

II Corinthians 11:14

Guadalupe

"A shrine of the blessed virgin in central Mexico, scene of the apparition of our lady to a native Aztec peasant. Her message: 'You must know, and be very certain in your heart, my son, that I am truly the eternal virgin, Holy Mother of the true God." [194]

Siluva
(Jesus appears as a sleeping child)

"Lithuanian shrine to the weeping virgin, to which over a hundred thousand formerly came annually to pray to Mary—A few shepherd children saw the vision of a beautiful young woman holding a sleeping child in her arms, dressed in white, she was crying, her tears falling on her little one." [195]

After his resurrection, Jesus appeared to Mary Magdalene, Mary the mother of Jesus, Salome, the apostles, and many disciples. The Bible records two subsequent appearances, but not exactly as a "sleeping child."

No more baby Jesus

As he neared Damascus on his journey, suddenly a light from heaven flashed around him. He fell to the ground and heard a voice say to him, 'Saul, Saul, why do you persecute me?' 'Who are you Lord?' Saul asked. 'I am Jesus, who you are persecuting,' he replied. 'Now get up and go into the city, and you will be told what you must do.' Saul got up from the ground, but when he opened his eyes he could see nothing, so they led him by the hand into Damascus. For three days he was blind.

Acts 9:3-9

I turned around to see the voice that was speaking to me. And when I turned I saw seven golden lampstands, and someone 'like a son of man' dressed in a robe reaching down to his feet and with a golden sash around his chest. His head and hair were white like wool, as white as snow, and his eyes were like blazing fire. His feet were like bronze in a furnace, and his voice was like the sound of rushing water. In his right hand he held seven stars, and out of his mouth came a sharp double edged sword. His face was like the sun shining in all its brilliance. When I saw him, I fell at his feet as though dead.

Revelation 1:12-17

5

Mystery
Babylon the Great
Revelation 17

"The writer of a good mystery drops clues throughout the play, some meaningful, as it turns out later, some down rabbit trails leading nowhere,--but as the end of the play nears, secrets are revealed, story lines converge, important clues are confirmed as such, and the mystery is solved." [196]

No more rabbit trails

When the book of Revelation was written circa 96 A.D., "Babylon the Great, the Mother of Prostitutes," would certainly have been a mystery to the church of the first century. However, by the third century the mystery would begin to unfold. As we near the end of the play, many secrets have been revealed, story lines have converged, and important clues have been confirmed.

Today, as never before in our history we can compare the teachings and claims of Catholicism against the truth of scripture and the facts of history and expose the church of Rome.

The Great Prostitute

"The hierarchy had divorced itself from Christ, the savior of the human race, in order to fornicate with all his torturers." [197]

"Politics and religion could not have been more intricately intertwined." [198]

"JohnVIII advanced the cause of the papal supremacy by successfully asserting the right of the popes not only to crown but also to choose the emperor." [199]

"Hildabrand's (Pope Gregory VII) dream finally materialized, there was now a new papacy symbolized by the right of the popes to wear the imperial signia, including the tiara, a conical shaped headdress with a crown. The pope indeed was now a world leader and would dominate the life of Europe—both spiritual and temporal for centuries." [200]

"The successors of Martin V in the 15th century and the first half of the 16th century, were chiefly interested in increasing the temporal power of the papacy, in patronizing the arts and letters, in beautifying the city, and in raising the fortunes of themselves and their relatives, the moral tone of the papal court was scandal to Christendom." [201]

With her the kings of the earth committed adultery.

Revelation 17:2

"The division between church and state was so slight that the emperor had a right to approve who could enter a religious community or order." [202]

"Constantine considered himself not the pope, to be the leading figure of the church." [203]

"In Constantine's view, the security of the empire and the unity of the church were inseparably linked. Emperors and kings competed with church leaders for control of the church, its personnel, its beliefs, and its property—the papacy became central in the struggle over whether civil leaders or church leaders would control the church—later emperors continued to interfere in church life both in Rome and around the empire, sometimes the emperors had theological views they wanted imposed out of conviction, as when the empress Theodora used her money and influence to make Vigilus Pope in 537 after he promised to reject the Council of Chalcedon." [204]

Caesaropapism

"A term used primarily of the relationship between church and state in the Byzantine Empire, wherein the church tended to be a department of state, government controlled; the emperor was esteemed to have a sacred and quasi sacramental character: and so Caesar came almost to have the place of pope." [205]

"The old cannon law that required that a bishop be elected by clergy and people was completely forgotten—actual control over the appointment was seized by the king and his great vassals." [206]

"The height of earthly power in the church came under Innocent III, all rulers and noblemen were subjected to the pope and looked to him for help. For example, when the papal states were being invaded with their aid came conditions. One of the conditions was that the emperor of the Holy Roman Empire would be in attendance at papal elections. Rulers also had a say in who could be bishops in their realm." [207]

"Another ominous development was the monopoly acquired by the nobility over the high offices of the church. It was quite common for a prince to have his younger sons appointed to bishoprics as the only way of securing a style of living appropriate to their station. Between 1450 and 1520 no fewer than five ducal princes were bishops and two of them only eight years old at the time of their nomination." [208]

The woman dressed in purple and scarlet,

Revelation 17:4

"Vestments come in liturgical colors: purple or violet: a symbol of penance and reparation. It is used during the penitent seasons of advent and lent and at the celebration of the sacrament of penance. It may also be used at funeral masses and all souls day observances." [209]

"The color of blood is used on all feasts of our Lord's cross and passion, including Palm Sunday and on the feasts of the apostles and all martyrs. Red is also used on Pentecost and in masses of the Holy Spirit, in memory of the tongues of fire of the first Pentecost." [210]

"The bishops of Rome wore cardinal robes of scarlet red—Cardinals wear scarlet red to represent their willingness to die for the pope.—A biretta is a special cap of three corners and ridges worn by clerics."—"A red biretta with no pom-pom is for a cardinal." [211]

Glittering with gold

Revelation 17:4

"Vestments made of gold damask material are permitted in place of white and are usually worn for the Christmas season, All Saints, Christ the King, and Feast of the Blood of Christ." [212]

The Chalice: "For centuries it was made of precious material; if it was not gold, the interior of the cup was gold plated." [213]

"A gold ring with a stone worn upon the third finger of the right hand is part of the insignia of office of cardinals, bishops, and abbots, and kissed as a sign of respect." [214]

Ciborium: "Used for small communion hosts of the faithful, it is made of various precious metals—the interior is commonly gold or gold plated." [215]

Luna: " A circular receptacle with glass sides, metal circled with gold or gilded metal to hold the sacred host upright in the monstrance." [216]

The Golden Rose: "An ornament made of gold in imitation of a spray of roses. The device is solemnly blessed by the pope."—"The golden rose thus blessed is conferred from time to time on sovereigns and others." [217]

Precious stones

Revelation 17:4

"The pectoral cross is made of precious metal and is often embellished with precious or semi-precious jewels—usually extended on a gold chain." [218]

Tiara: "Papal crown, which is a tall headdress of gold cloth ornaments with precious stones." [219]

"The place where they worshipped had no particular importance, it was usually just a large room in one of the members homes. As time passed the Eucharist was no longer consecrated on a simple table but on a massive and ornate altar made of precious marbles and studded with gems." [220]

Pearls

Revelation 17:4

"The altar, which only the pope may use, is inlaid with mother pearl." [221]

She held a golden cup in her hand, filled with abominable things and the filth of her adulteries.

Revelation 17:4

The Chalice: "A cup of precious metal (the inside must be gold or gold plated) that holds the wine consecrated at mass which becomes the precious blood." [222]

The Catholic dictionary defines the chalice as; "The cup shaped vessel or goblet used at mass to contain the precious blood of Christ (for centuries it was made of precious material; if it was not gold, the interior of the cup was gold plated). A chalice is consecrated with holy chrism (holy oil) by a bishop." [223]

"Just as he did with the host, the priest lifts the chalice and shows it to the people. After he has blessed it...during the middle ages chalices were generally wider than those used today, and hence more difficult to hold aloft in due reverence." [224]

"After the consecration but before holy communion, the priest places a small piece of the host into the precious blood in the chalice—every minute piece of the host, every drop of the precious blood is the whole risen savior. How this all happens is a mystery of faith." [225]

"The Council of Trent in the sixteenth century defined that only the priest had to consume both to complete the sacrament. The faithful could just receive the sacred host and not the chalice of precious blood since either one is both of them (body and blood of Christ)." [226]

Mystery Babylon the Great

Revelation 17:5

She who is in Babylon chosen together with you sends you her greetings.

I Peter 5:13

Peter the apostle, writing from Rome about A.D, 66 unambiguously refers to Rome as Babylon.

I saw the woman was drunk with the blood of the saints, the blood of those who bore testimony to Jesus.

Revelation 17:6

A Gospel you can't Refuse

Catholic apologists: "How should a Catholic answer charge about the Inquisition? He should not deny the undeniable." [227]

"Ask fundamentalists just what they think the inquisitor's existence demonstrates. They wouldn't bring it up in the first place unless they thought it proves something about the Catholic Church. Just what is that something." [228]

Catholic apologists have a much bigger problem regarding the Inquisition than simply not denying the undeniable. How do you explain to the faithful that they are bound by the doctrine and teaching of men who possessed the moral integrity and spirituality of Genghis Khan? The 'something' that the Inquisition so clearly and unequivocally demonstrates is this:

> *The time is coming that whoever kills you will think he is offering a service to God. They will do such things because they have not known the Father or me.*

John 16: 2,3

Nothing in the history of western civilization bears greater witness to the Church of Rome's human depravity and religious hypocrisy than the Inquisition!

In a continuing and never ending effort to distance herself from the atrocities of the Inquisition, the Church of Rome continues to obfuscate and water down the historical facts regarding the most terrible engine of tyranny ever created by man: Catholic apologists: "The institution was based on the principle that truth must be upheld and promoted in the interest of secular no less than ecclesiastical justice; error must be abandoned or uprooted. The Inquisition was punctilious in its adherence to law." [229]

"The Inquisition established in Spain was purely a state tribunal."—"It is true that abuses crept in, but this is no reason for criminating the church." [230]

Renowned authors and church historians: "It was the popes themselves who invented the Inquisition and saw that it was carried out. Gregory IX, in 1233, handed over the office (of the Inquisition) in permanence to the Dominicans, but always to be exercised in the name, and by the authority of the pope." [231]

"Of eighty popes in a line from the thirteenth century on, not one of them disapproved of the theology and apparatus of the Inquisition. On the contrary, one after another added his own cruel touches to the workings of this deadly machine." [232]

The Waldenses of France
Circa A.D. 1200

"Peter Waldo, a rich merchant of Lyons, sold all his goods, gave the money to the poor, and went out to preach the gospel in the way that he believed it should be taught. Waldo soon had many followers, and it is said he made for their use a translation of the New Testament into the French language. He and his preachers travelled from place to place, exhorting the people to lead better lives, and telling them to turn to the scriptures for knowledge to bring them to salvation, rather than to the priests. Word of what was happening soon came to Rome, and the pope sent out an order forbidding any person to preach without first receiving authority from him. It was the preaching of Waldo and his followers that first brought about the appointment of 'inquisitors' (questioners or examiners) by the Roman Church." [233]

Dear friends, let us love one another, for love comes from God.
Everyone who loves has been born of God and knows God.
Whoever does not love does not know God.

I John 4:7,8

The Love of the Dominican Friars

"A priest named Dominic, who instituted an order called the order of Dominican Friars: The members of which community have ever since been the principal inquisitors in every country into which that terrible tribunal has been introduced. Their power was unlimited; they proceeded against whom they pleased, without any regard for age, sex, or rank. However infamous the accusers, the charge was listened to, and even unsigned letters were thought sufficient evidence to occasion arrest. The dearest friends or relatives could not, without danger, serve anyone who was imprisoned on account of religion. To carry to those who were confined a little straw, or to give them a cup of water, was called favoring the heretics. No lawyer dared to plead for even his own brother. The vengeance of this merciless brotherhood pursued its victims beyond the grave, for the very bones of dead Waldenses were dug up and burned." [234]

*This is my command. Love each other: If the world hates you
keep in mind that it hated me first.*

Albigenses

The Albigenses were people who lived in Southern France. "Like the Waldenses, they had changed their form of religious worship from that of the Church of Rome, it is supposed they held opinions which bore some resemblance to those of Protestants of a later day, in as much as they seem to have refused to acknowledge the authority of Roman priests to stand between them and their God.

"Messengers were accordingly sent throughout the whole of Europe by Pope Innocent III to raise a force of soldiers large enough to utterly destroy the Albigenses for they had increased greatly in number and wealth. Promises of pardon for sins of the past, and indulgences in the future were freely offered by the pope, as bribes, to influence all who would take part in the so called holy war." [235]

"They were hunted through the streets by brutal soldiers, and no mercy was shown to man, woman or child, Thousands fell before swords and spears of these bloodthirsty foes, who revenged themselves for the siege by every kind of outrage and cruelty." [236]

*No servant is greater than his master. If they persecuted me, they
will persecute you also.*

John 15: 20

More persecution of the Waldenses

"It has already been told how some of those people called Waldenses left their native country, France, and went to live in the Northern part of Italy, where they were attacked by soldiers sent from Rome, and many of them killed." [237]

"The Waldenses were continually persecuted and pursued like wild animals by the Church of Rome. Their major crimes: "Purgatory was denied; to take oaths or to go to war was unlawful;

righteous laymen could absolve and preach; evil priests could not minister validly; (and last but certainly not least), the pope was repudiated." [238]

The Catholic Dictionary: "Condemned by Pope Lucius III, they became a threat to civil authority and were opposed by political rulers." [239]

"All sorts of accusations were then made against the Waldenses by the archbishop (of Turin); so in order to learn the real truth of the matter, the duke sent twelve of his officers into the valleys to find out what was the character of the people who lived there. After travelling through their towns and villages, and talking with the Waldenses, the twelve examiners returned to the duke, and gave him a most favorable account of them. They reported that the people appeared to be inoffensive, industrious, and pious."—"The duke therefore talked with these people, examined their children, and satisfied himself that the report of the commission was true.

"He then commanded the prelates who had attempted to deceive him, to depart from his court; and gave strict orders that the persecution should cease throughout his dominions." [240]

These were all commended for their faith, yet none of them received what had been promised, God had planned something better.

Hebrews 11:39

Paul III

"...gave orders to the Council at Turin to send messengers to the Waldenses to offer them the following hard terms: 'They must return to the Church of Rome.' It was threatened that if they rejected these propositions, persecution and death should be their penalty.

"The Waldenses response to the pope: 'No power could force them to renounce their religion—for they considered their souls far more precious than their bodies—this defiant reply so enraged the council that they seized all the Waldenses who ventured out from their mountain hiding places, and put them to death in the most cruel ways." [241]

They wandered in deserts and mountains, and in caves and holes in the ground.

Hebrews 11:38

"In the year 1650, a jubilee was held at Rome, and it was, as usual, a season for exciting renewed activity against all who opposed Romish doctrines.

"At that time the council, 'for destroying heretics' established courts in the principle cities of France and Italy.

"All the inhabitants of Lucerne, and the more open districts, were commanded to leave their homes and to retire to the mountains within three days, unless they became Romanists." [242]

"They gave up their dwellings and wading through the snow, with difficulty crossed the torrents, sheltering themselves in caves and under jutting rocks." [243]

Some faced jeers and flogging, while still others were chained and put in prison. They were stoned, they were sawed in two, they were put to death by the sword, they went about in sheepskins and goatskins, destitute, persecuted and mistreated.

Hebrews 11:36, 37

"In a few days the signal for a general massacre was given, and the most cruel torments were inflicted upon all who, trusting to the professions of peace, had not hidden themselves in the steepest and loftiest parts of the mountains—more than twelve thousand men and women were shut up in gloomy dungeons, and experienced the most cruel treatment." [244]

(The Not So) Innocent III (1198-1216)

The launching pad for one of the most terrible engines of tyranny ever created by man, "the most holy father," Innocent III, he was the first pope to apply force on a considerable scale to suppress religious opinions." [245]

"Innocent, perceiving that the Waldenses, and other sects differing from the church were increasing in numbers, sent among them inquisitors, or monks who were known to be devoted to the cause of the church, As their name implied, they were appointed to inquire into everything that might lead to the discovery of heresy." [246]

"Among his accomplishments, as the 'Vicar of Christ:' he could call upon great sums of money to buy, and to bribe back the lands he believed belonged to the Roman See. The papacy became wealthy during his tenure of office. He rebuilt the Lateran and Vatican palaces; he provided the impoverished Archbishop of Ravenna with liturgical vestments. Innocent himself revised the imperial coronation ritual to include the popes girding the sword onto the emperor, as a sign that it was the papacy which gave the emperor his temporal authority. He was obsessed with the crusading ideal, and preached or authorized six of them during his reign." [247]

"As Vicar of Christ—a title he was the first pope to adopt—he had made and unmade kings and emperors—his pontificate mark the high point in the papacy." [248]

"Until 1248, inquisitors had no buildings of their own, but traveled about from place to place; after that date they began to have houses called courts of the inquisition, in which they lived and in which they could try, torture, and imprison those who fell under suspicion of holding views contrary to the Church of Rome."[249]

The Spanish Inquisition

"In the year 1480, it was established with the consent of Ferdinand and Isabella, and became more powerful and was more dreaded than any court that had ever before existed in the world. Woe to the men or women forced to enter the gloomy portals of the Spanish Inquisition—a fate worse than death awaited them.

"The profit, or spoils, wrung from its victims amounted to large sums annually, and this was divided between the king, and the Church of Rome. All the officials of the holy office, as the inquisition was called, were also paid from the confiscated property of the accused; it was therefore to the interest of each one of them that the stream of wealth should not run dry." [250]

The Dominican 'Fryer' Torquemada

"The increasing activity of the holy office soon required a more efficient body of workers; so the Dominican monk, Thomas of Torquemada, a name that will be forever infamous in history, was made inquisitor general by Pope Sixtus IV.

"Torquemada was chief inquisitor until his death, and during the eighteen years he ruled the holy office, ten thousand two hundred and twenty persons were burned alive, and ninety-seven thousand three hundred and seventy-two punished with loss of property, or imprisonment—numbers so large as to seem incredible, but which are given by Llorente, the Spanish historian of the Inquisition, who was well qualified to judge of the accuracy." [251]

Pius V extends cruelties of the Inquisition to ships at sea: "Not satisfied with encouraging the Inquisition to practice its cruelties on the land, Phillip II established it even upon his ships at sea.

"It is recorded that in 1571, a large fleet having been drawn together, under the command of John of Austria, and manned with soldiers of various nations, Phillip, with the consent of Pope Pius V, to prevent any corruption of the faith, deputed one of the Spanish inquisitors to discharge the duties of his office at sea." [252]

The Heretic Galileo
(Renowned astronomer and physicist)

"After a long and bitter review of Galileo's writings, in which many of his most important discoveries were condemned as errors, the charge of the inquisitors went on to declare, 'That you, Galileo, have upon account of those things which you have written and confessed, subjected yourself to a strong suspicion of heresy in this holy office, by believing, and holding to be true a doctrine which is false, and contrary to the sacred divine scripture—in order to save his life, Galileo admitted that he was wrong." [253]

The Huguenots

"In France the 'spirit of rebellion' against the church had been nurtured by the Huguenots." [254]

"For centuries France had been the battleground of the Roman church and the sects opposed to it. We have seen how the Waldenses and the Albigenses suffered in the struggle; the cities were taken, their homes destroyed, and themselves slain by thousands; so that only a few scattered remnants remained of a once numerous and prosperous people—they had previously been content to meet in secret, to sing hymns, and listen to earnest prayer and practical preaching in some lowly shelter that would not awaken the suspicions of their enemies.

"The first French Huguenot church in Paris was established in the year 1555, and almost immediately afterword there sprang up fifteen other congregations each having pastors, elders, and deacons. And each ruling itself and recognizing no bond of fellowship except that of charity and sufferings. [255]

The Massacre of the 'Spirit of Rebellion'
St Bartholomew

"Paris resounded with savage yells and howls which brought multitudes of terror-stricken people out of their lodging places, not only unarmed, but many of them half dressed—bands of murderers swept the streets in all directions, killing everyone they met, From the streets they rushed into the houses; they broke open the doors, and spared neither age, sex, nor condition. Even some priests took part in the bloody work; and going ahead of the murderers urged them, in God's name, to spare none. When daylight appeared, Paris presented a most appalling scene of slaughter. Headless bodies were hanging from the windows; gateways were blocked up with the dead and dying; and whole streets were filled with mutilated corpses.

"Even the palace of the Louvre was the scene of great carnage; the guards were drawn up around it, and the unfortunate in the palace were called out, one after another, and killed with the soldiers halberts, most of them died without complaining or even speaking. The massacre lasted during the whole week. On Tuesday a proclamation was issued for putting an end to it, but no measures were taken for enforcing the order." [256]

The 'Rebellious' Huguenots flee to a prison for refuge

"During the confusion and uproar of that fatal night, seven or eight hundred panic-stricken people sought refuge in the prison, hoping thus to escape from the fierce bands who ravaged the streets. But armed guards, who had been placed there for that very purpose, drove the poor fugitives out into an open courtyard, where they were slain with swords and clubs.

"The number of persons who were killed in the massacre, in the city of Paris, was over four thousand. From Paris the order went forth to the cities of France, 'Slay the Huguenots!' And within a few days thousands of additional lives had been sacrificed." [257]

The 'Spirit of Rebellion' persists

"Now Leonard Morel, the minister, had just begun his sermon, and some hundred or more men and women were listening to his words, when the reports of two muskets sounded in their ears. The people frightened at this, tried to escape by the door, but were driven back by the soldiers, who rushed in upon them crying out, 'Death to the Huguenots!'

"The massacre at the church continued for nearly an hour. There were killed in this attack sixty persons, besides seven others who died afterward from their wounds." [258]

Orleans

"A dreadful massacre of the Huguenots took place at the city of Orleans. All through the night nothing could be heard but the firing of guns and pistols, the breaking down of doors and the despairing screams of women and children." [259]

Toulouse

"Nearly three hundred of the Huguenots were murdered at Toulouse, and after being stripped of their clothing, their bodies were exposed to public view for two days, and then thrown into great pits." [260]

Bordeaux

"The massacre at Bordeaux was begun and carried on in much the same manner as the others. But many of the Huguenots found means to escape from the city, and hid themselves among the rocks and marshes until they had an opportunity to sail for England." [261]

Sancerre

"The city of Sancerre, which was inhabited chiefly by Huguenots, many of whom had fled there for safety, was besieged by the kings army. Having but a scanty supply of provisions the people soon began to suffer from hunger, and were forced to eat the flesh of horses and dogs. During the hardships of the siege almost all aged persons and children died. Hunger killed at least five hundred." [262]

At last the 'Spirit of Rebellion' is squelched

"All their minsters and principle men were ordered to leave France; only a few days being allowed them in which to depart. Many were purposely detained by their enemies, or were unable to find means to travel; and these were condemned to the galleys, or convict ships. They were collected together in prisons; fed only on bread and water, and then marched off to the seacoast in large companies, hand cuffed and chained together.

"At a later date some of the Huguenots came to the United States, and these, likewise, added much to the prosperity of the communities among whom they settled. They were noted for their morality, integrity, and business enterprise." [263]

"The 'Spirit of Rebellion' nurtured by the Huguenots against the Church of Rome was in reality a spirit that refused to submit to the sovereign religious authority of a man who claimed to be the supreme ruler of all Christians. It was a spirit that rejected false doctrine, the gospel of sacramental grace, and temporal and spiritual tyranny; it was in truth a spirit that bore testimony to Jesus!

"By 1808, when the Inquisition was abolished, its victims numbered, according to the historian named before (Llorente); 31,912 persons burned alive, and 291,450 imprisoned in its dungeons." [264]

Seven hills on which the woman sits.

Revelation 17:9

Rome: "The seven hills of the ancient city are the Palatine, roughly in the center with the Capitaline to the northwest and the Quirinal, Viminal, Esquiline, Caelian, and Aventine in an outlying north southwest curve." [265]

The waters you saw, where the prostitute sits, are peoples, multitudes, nations and languages.

Revelation 17:15

"The Catholic church which sets out to teach the whole world, which is now in fact worldwide in extension and inclusion of men of all races and cultures." [266]

"There are over one billion Catholics in the world today, spread over every continent, speaking almost every conceivable language, and all answering to a single authority." [267]

Revelation 18

I sit as queen, I am not a widow and I will never mourn.

Revelation 18:7

I will continue forever—the eternal queen.

Isaiah 47:7 (Babylon)

I am and there is none besides me.

Isaiah 47:8 (Babylon)

"All the faithful of Christ must believe that the apostolic see and the Roman pontiff hold primacy over the whole world."

"Indefectibility is an attribute of the Catholic church. It means the church will endure forever until the end of time nothing can destroy it. Even the Borgia and Medici scandals, and the recent sex scandals in the USA, have hurt, but not destroyed, the Catholic Church." [268]

Woe! Woe, O great city dressed in fine linen.

Revelation 18:16

"Altar linens are the many beautiful sacramentals centering on the holy sacrifice of the mass.

"The purificator: A small linen cloth used by the priest on the altar at the beginning of mass.

"Amice: A square white linen wrapped around the neck and covering the shoulders.

"Alb: A long white linen garment reaching to the feet." [269]

By your magic spell all the nations were led astray.

Revelation 18:23

Keep on with your magic spells and with your many sorceries.

Isaiah 47: 12 (Babylon)

Eucharisticum Mysterium
The magic spell of the Eucharist [270]

"The priest separately consecrates the wafers of (wheat) bread and then separately consecrates the chalice of (grape) wine to symbolize the separation of body and blood, so he can sacramentally re-enact the sacrifice of Calvary where Jesus shed his blood and was crucified in his body, yet it is not dead flesh and blood which is received in holy communion but the risen body and blood of Christ." [271]

The Great Abomination

"The priest speaks and lo! Christ, the eternal and omnipotent God, bows his head in humble obedience to the priests command." [272]

The Eucharistic sacrifice of the mass is the greatest religious hoax ever perpetrated on a lost and dying world. To teach that Christ conferred on an elite and royal priesthood of sinful men the power to make him present himself under the appearance of bread and wine so that they may sacrifice him and ingest him like a one-a-day spiritual vitamin, is nothing short of an abomination!

6

Conclusion

Catholics who love Jesus need to know that when they embrace doctrine like the Eucharistic sacrifice of the mass and the gospel of sacramental grace, they unwittingly tell Christ that his excruciating death on a cross for our sins and the sin of the whole world was okay but it needs some work, it can be improved!

If you belong to a church comprised of sinful men who claim to be superior because they are Christ's official representatives, divinely appointed by God to dispense his grace, your best bet is to head for the nearest exit.

If you are being held captive by an institution that claims divine revelation regarding Christ's *insufficient* atoning sacrifice for our sins, I implore you to heed the prophetic words of Revelation 18:4:

Come out of her my people.

Notes

1. "The Vatican Exposed" Williams, Prometheus, 03

2. A Concise History of the Catholic Church, Bokenkotter, page 111

3. A Concise History of the Catholic Church, page 46

4. 'Adoration' Catholic Dictionary, Hardon

5. A Concise History of the Catholic Church page 36

6. 'Patrimony of St. Peter' Catholic Dictionary; Hardon, Attwater

7. Fox's Christian Martyrs, Page 234

8. Columbia Encyclopedia, page 2439 'pope'

9. Catholicism Answer Book, Trigilio, Brighenti (110)

10. Peter in Rome, D W O'Connor, Columbia Press, 207

11. Columbia Encyclopedia, Papacy, 2139

12. A Concise History of the Catholic Church, 84

13. Catholicism Answer Book, 377

14. Ibid, 129

15. Catholic Dictionary, Attwater, "Schism of the West"

16. Ibid, "Schism"

17. Ibid

18. History of the Popes, O'Malley

19. Inside the Vatican: The Politics and Organization of the Catholic Church, Reese, 88

20. A concise History of the Catholic Church, 192

21. A Concise History of the Catholic Church, 198

22. Ibid, 202

23. Ibid, 42

24. The Popes, Walsh; 36, 41, 42, 43

25. The Popes, Walsh; 43, 44

26. A History of the Popes, O'Malley; 36

27. The Popes, Walsh; 53

28. The Popes, Walsh; 55, 57

29. The Popes, Walsh; 55, 57

30. The Decline and Fall of the Roman Church, Martin; 115

31. History of the Popes, O'Malley; 73

32. Catholicism Answer Book, 257

33. The Decline and Fall of the Roman Church, Martin; 110

34. History of the Popes, O'Malley; 73

35. Inside the Vatican, Reese; 291

36. Ibid 80

37. The Decline and Fall of the Roman Church, Martin; 110

38. History of the Popes, O'Malley; 83

39. The Decline and Fall of the Roman Church, Martin; 126

40. The Popes, Walsh; 93

41. The Popes, Walsh; 93

42. Papacy,' Columbia Encyclopedia, 6th

43. History of the Popes; 87

44. The Popes, Walsh; 97

45. The Decline and Fall of the Roman Church, Martin; 132

46. The Popes, Walsh; 98

47. Inside the Vatican, Reese; 100

48. A Concise History of the Catholic Church; 131

49. Catholicism Answer Book; 284

50. Catholicism Answer Book; 285

51. The Decline and Fall of the Roman Church, Martin; 175

52. Ibid 180

53. The Inquisition of the Middle Agres, Lea; 315

54. A History of the Popes, O'Malley; 149. 150

55. A Concise History of the Catholic Church; 187

56. The Decline and Fall of the Roman Church, Martin; 184

57. Rich Church, Poor Church, Martin;190

58. The Decline and Fall of the Roman Church, Martin; 190

59. Catholicism Answer Book, 310

60. The Decline and Fall of the Roman Church, Martin; 191

61. Catholicism Answer Book, 311

62. Columbia Encyclopedia, 6th; 2439

63. Catholicism Answer Book, 377

64. A History of the Popes, O'Malley; 174-175

65. Ibid; 176

66. A History of the Popes, O'Malley; 176

67. A Gospel of Shame, Burkett, Bruni; 128

68. A History of the Popes, O'Malley; 179

69. A Concise History of the Catholic Church; 216

70. The Decline and Fall of the Roman Church, Martin; 200-201, 2003

71. The Inquisition of the Middle Ages, Lea; 315

72. A History of the Popes, O'Malley; 190, 192, 198

73. Ibid, 202, 203

74. A History of the Popes, O'Malley; 204

75. A Concise History of the Catholic Church; 246

76. Ibid, 202

77. Columbia Encyclopedia, 6th; 2439

78. How the Pope Became Infallible, Hasler, Doubleday, 1981; 118, 124

79. Papal Sins, Wills, Doubleday; 40, 41

80. A Concise History of the Catholic Church; 386-387

81. Ibid, 387-389

82. Catholic Church and Nazi Germany, Lewy; 336

83. A Concise History of the Catholic Church; 391

84. The Vatican Exposed,

85. A Concise History of the Catholic Church; 435-436

86. Catholicism Answer Book, Trigilio, Brighenti; 377

87. Ibid, 310-311

88. Ibid, 375

89. Canons Ecclesiastical Catholic Dictionary, Attwater

90. Catholicism Answer Book, Trigilio, Brighenti; 109

91. ' Sacraments' Catholic Dictionary, Hardon, Attwater

92. 'Grace' Catholic Dictionary, Hardon, Attwater

93. Catholicism Answer Book, Trigilio, Brighenti; 88

94. 'Sacraments' Catholic Dictionary, Hardon, Attwater

95. Catholicism Answer Book, Trigilio, Brighenti; 73

96. 'Limbo' Catholic Dictionary, Hardon, Attwater

97. Catholicism Answer Book, Trigilio, Brighenti; 193

98. A Concise History of the Catholic Church, 423

99. Catholicism Answer Book; Trigilo, Brighenti; 310, 311

100. Catholicism Answer Book, Trigilio, Brighenti; 74

101. Ibid

102. Ibid

103. 'Water'—The American Heritage Dictionary, Second College Edition

104. The Manual of the Holy Catholic Church, JJ McGovern

105. Catholicism Answer Book, Trigilio, Brighenti; 147

106. 'Transubstantiation' Catholic Dictionary, Hardon

107. A Concise History of the Catholic Church; 43, taken from the writings of Justin Martyr, an early church father 165 A.D.

108. A Concise History of the Catholic Church; 54

109. Ibid, 145-146

110. A Concise History of the Catholic Church; 145-146

111. A Concise History of the Catholic Church; 200

112. A Concise History of the Catholic Church; 358,147

113. 'Mass' Catholic Dictionary, Hardon

114. Catholicism Answer Book, Trigilio, Brighenti; 146-147

115. 'The Mass' Rops, 121,125

116. Ibid 122

117. 'The Mass' Rops, 121, 125

118. The Faith of Millions: the credentials of the Catholic Religion, John Obrien; 255, 256 (as reported in our 'Sun day Visitor,' 1974

119. Ibid

120. 'Purgatory' Catholic Dictionary, Hardon

121. 'Purgatory' The American Heritage Dictionary, Second College Edition

122. 'Purgatory' Catholic Dictionary, Hardon

123. The Manual of the Holy Catholic Church, JJ McGovern; 316

124. The Divine Teaching Authority of the Catholic Church

125. 'Indulgence' Catholic Dictionary, Hardon

126. Rich Church, Poor Church, Martin; 18, 126

127. 'Immaculate Conception and Assumption' Catholic Answers Tract; PO Box 17181, San Diego, CA 17181

128. 'Hyperdouleia' Catholic Dictionary, Hardon

129. 'Petrus Romanus,' Horn, Putnam; 330

130. Columbia Encyclopedia, 6th; 1177

131. A Dictionary of World Mythology, Cotterell; 161

132. Papal Sins, Wills; 206

133. Papal Sins, Wills; 210-211

134. Catholicism Answer Book, Trigilio, Brighenti; 59,60

135. How the Pope Became Infallible, Hasler; 118-129

136. Immaculate Conception, Attwater

137. 'Structures of Deceit,' Papal Sin, Wills; 254

138. 'Immaculate Conception' Catholic Dictionary, Hardon

139. History of the Popes, O'Malley; 244

140. 'Immaculate Conception' Catholic Dictionary, Hardon

141. As cited in 'Petrus Romanus', Horn, Putnum; 327, 328

142. Ibid

143. 'Infallibility' Catholic Dictionary, Hardon

144. 'Infallibility' Catholic Dictionary, Hardon

145. 'Assumption' Catholic Dictionary, Hardon

146. Catholicism Answer Book, Trigilio, Brighenti; 64, 65

147. Catholicism Answer Book, Trigilio, Brighenti; 64, 65

148. 'Dogma' Catholic Dictionary, Hardon

149. Papal Sin, 206

150. Papal Sin, 206

151. 'Ad Diem Illum' Catholic Dictionary, Hardon

152. 'Mediatrix' Catholic Dictionary, Hardon

153. Ibid

154. Catholicism Answer Book, Trigilio, Brighenti; 58

155. 'Mariolatry' Catholic Dictionary, Hardon

156. Catholicism Answer Book, Trigilio, Brighenti; 248

157. 'Prayer to our lady of Mount Carmel,' Catholic Shrines of Western Europe, Wright

158. Prayer of Pope Pius XII, as cited in 'Petrus Romanus', Horn, Putnam; 331-332

159. 'The Glories of Mary,' St. Alphonsus de Liquor, Redemptorist Fathers, 1931; 171, as cited in "A Woman Rides the Beast," Hunt; 434

160. 'Marian Art', Catholic Dictionary, Hardon

161. 'Marianists' Catholic Dictionary, Hardon

162. 'Mariology' Catholic Dictionary, Hardon

163. 'Marists' Catholic Dictionary, Hardon

164. Marion Literature' Catholic Dictionary, Hardon; quote from John Huskin, Catholic author

165. 'Consecration to Mary' Catholic Dictionary, Hardon

166. Papal Sins, Wills; 208

167. 'Shrines' Attwater

168. Papal Sins, Wills; 211

169. Catholicism Answer Book, Trigilio, Brighenti; 67

170. Ibid

171. 'Fatima' Catholic Dictionary, Hardon

172. 'Immaculate Heart' Catholic Dictionary, Hardon

173. Catholic Shrines of Western Europe, Wright; 192

174. Ibid, 193

175. 'Fatima' Catholic Dictionary, Hardon

176. 'Banneux' Catholic Dictionary, Hardon

177. Catholic Shrines of Western Europe, Wright; (Banneux)

178. Ibid, "Our Lady of Beauraing"

179. 'Laus' Catholic Dictionary, Hardon

180. Catholic Shrines of Western Europe, Wright; (Lourdes)

181. Catholicism Answer Book, Trigilio, Brighenti; 324

182. 'Zoce' Catholic Dictionary, Hardon

183. 'Czestochowa' Catholic Dictionary, Hardon

184. Catholic Shrines of Western Europe, Wright; 82

185. 'Prayer to our Lady of Pellevoisin' Ibid

186. 'Copacabana' Catholic Dictionary, Hardon

187. 'Divine Love' Catholic Dictionary, Hardon

188. 'Saragosa' Ibid

189. 'Africa' Ibid

190. 'Mokameh' Catholic Dictionary, Hardon

191. 'Panaya Kapula' Ibid

192. 'Holy Days' 'All Saints' Catholic Dictionary, Hardon

193. Catholicism Answer Book, Trigilio, Brighenti; 212

194. 'Guadalupe' Catholic Dictionary, Hardon

195. 'Siluva' Catholic Dictionary, Hardon

196. The End of America, Price, Christian House, 43

197. A Concise History of the Catholic Church; 301

198. A History of the Popes, O'Malley; 184

199. A Concise History of the Catholic Church; 111

200. Ibid, 120

201. Columbia Encyclopedia, 6th; 2439

202. Catholicism Answer Book, Trigilio, Brighenti; 288

203. Inside the Vatican, Reese; 27

204. Inside the Vatican, Reese; 451

205. 'Caesaropapism', Catholic Dictionary, Attwater

206. A Concise History of the Catholic Church; 114

207. Catholicism Answer Book, Trigilio, Brighenti; 288

208. A Concise History of the Catholic Church; 199

209. Catholicism Answer Book, Trigilio, Brighenti; 360

210. Ibid

211. Ibid 362

212. Catholicism Answer Book, Trigilio, Brighenti; 360

213. 'Chalice' Catholic Dictionary, Hardon

214. 'Ring' Catholic Dictionary, Attwater

215. 'Ciborium' Catholic Dictionary, Hardon

216. 'Luna' Catholic Dictionary, Hardon

217. 'Golden Rose' Catholic Dictionary, Attwater

218. Catholicism Answer Book, Trigilio, Brighenti; 363

219. 'Tiara' Catholic Dictionary, Hardon

220. A Concise History of the Catholic Church; 45

221. 'Sistine Chapel' Catholic Dictionary, Hardon

222. Catholicism Answer Book, Trigilio, Brighenti; 358

223. 'Chalice' Catholic Dictionary, Hardon

224. 'The Mass,' Rops; 122

225. Catholicism Answer Book, Trigilio, Brighenti; 151

226. Catholicism Answer Book, Trigilio, Brighenti; 355

227. Catholic Answers Tract, PO Box 17181, San Diego, CA 17181 'The Inquisition'

228. Ibid

229. 'Inquisition' Catholic Dictionary, Attwater

230. The Manual of the Holy Catholic Church, McGovern, 32, #101

231. 'The Papacy and the Civil Power' RW Thompson, NY 1876, 83 (as cited in 'The Woman Rides the Beast.')

232. De Rosa, opcit, 215, (as cited in 'A Woman Rides the Beast')

233. Foxe's Christian Martyrs of the World,' Moody, Chicago; 179-180

234. Foxe's Christian Martyrs of the World,' Moody, Chicago; 181

235. Foxe's Christian Martyrs of the World,' Moody, Chicago; 186-187

236. Foxe's Christian Martyrs of the World,' Moody, Chicago; 203

237. Foxe's Christian Martyrs of the World,' Moody, Chicago; 203

238. 'Waldensism' Catholic Dictionary, Attwater

239. 'Waldeneses' Catholicism Answer Book, Trigilio, Brighenti;

240. Foxe's Christian Martyrs of the World,' Moody, Chicago; 204-205

241. Foxe's Christian Martyrs of the World,' Moody, Chicago; 204-205

242. Foxe's Christian Martyrs of the World,' Moody, Chicago; 214

243. Foxe's Christian Martyrs of the World,' Moody, Chicago; 215

244. Foxe's Christian Martyrs of the World,' Moody, Chicago; 215

245. A Concise History of the Catholic Church; 131

246. Foxe's Christian Martyrs of the World,' Moody, Chicago; 231

247. The Popes, Walsh; St. Martins Press, NY; 112-114

248. The Popes, Walsh; St. Martins Press, NY; 118

249. Foxe's Christian Martyrs of the World,' Moody, Chicago; 231

250. Foxe's Christian Martyrs of the World,' Moody, Chicago; 232, 233

251. Foxe's Christian Martyrs of the World,' Moody, Chicago; 232, 233

252. Foxe's Christian Martyrs of the World,' Moody, Chicago; 258

253. Foxe's Christian Martyrs of the World,' Moody, Chicago; 258-259

254. The Manual of the Holy Catholic Church, McGovern, 324, 325

255. Foxe's Christian Martyrs of the World,' Moody, Chicago; 282, 283, 285

256. Foxe's Christian Martyrs of the World,' Moody, Chicago; 290-292

257. Foxe's Christian Martyrs of the World,' Moody, Chicago; 297

258. Foxe's Christian Martyrs of the World,' Moody, Chicago; 300, 303

259. Foxe's Christian Martyrs of the World,' Moody, Chicago; 303

260. Foxe's Christian Martyrs of the World,' Moody, Chicago; 305

261. Foxe's Christian Martyrs of the World,' Moody, Chicago; 306

262. Foxe's Christian Martyrs of the World,' Moody, Chicago; 307

263. Foxe's Christian Martyrs of the World,' Moody, Chicago; 312-313

264. Foxe's Christian Martyrs of the World,' Moody, Chicago; 234

265. 'Rome' Columbia Encyclopedia, 6th edition

266. 'Catholicity,' Catholic Dictionary, Attwater

267. 'Inside the Vatican,' Reese; Harvard University Press

268. Catholicism Answer Book, Trigilio, Brighenti; 310, 312

269. Catholicism Answer Book, Trigilio, Brighenti; 358, 359

270. 'Eucharisticum Mysterium' Catholic Dictionary, Hardon

271. Catholicism Answer Book, Trigilio, Brighenti; 355

272. John A. O'Brien, 'The Faith of Millions,' (as reported in 'Our Sunday Visitor')'The Credentials of the Catholic Religion,' 255-256

Made in the USA
Las Vegas, NV
31 March 2022